The Art of Management

for

Christian Leaders

The Art of Management for Christian Leaders

Ted W. Engstrom
and
Edward R. Dayton

Word Books, Publisher
Waco, Texas

The Art of Management for Christian Leaders

ISBN # 0–87680–473–3

Library of Congress catalog card number: 76–9563

Printed in the United States of America.

To all the men and women
of World Vision International
from whom we have learned so much.

Contents

List of Figures

Preface

As this book is finished the authors have known each other for ten years. In many ways we are two very different men. Ted Engstrom has moved through a series of responsibilities in the publishing industry and the leadership of Christian organizations. Ed Dayton has spent eighteen years in the aerospace industry before going to seminary and then joining World Vision in 1967. But we have learned a great deal from each other and from the people with whom it has been our privilege to work at World Vision.

Many of the ideas in the chapters that follow came out of the hours that we have spent together teaching management courses and seminars to thousands of Christian leaders. As it has been our privilege to be instructors, so it has also been our privilege to be learners.

In late 1972 the number of requests for information on a variety of topics had grown to such an extent that we felt that World Vision should begin a new ministry. Thus the *Christian Leadership Letter* was born. The contents of this book are primarily made up of these letters. They have been rearranged and edited. Some new reference material has been added.

We would be quick to admit that we are still learning. As World Vision has grown to a large Christian organization, we have had to manage in areas where neither of us had ever been before. It has been an exciting time, and even the more exciting because as men who are involved in the Lord's business we are able to walk into the future with the confidence that our times are in his hands.

It is our prayer that as you read this book that you will

gain some new insight of your own as to what kind of a leader God wants *you* to be.

Monrovia, California

Ted W. Engstrom
Edward R. Dayton

PART ONE

Leadership
in the Organization

1.

How to Get

Where You're Going

Are you a leader in a Christian organization that seems to be bogged down by its own weight? Are you frustrated by your inability to "get things moving"? Do you have a many-aimed organization that seems to be getting all tangled up in itself? Well, you're not alone. There are pastors, denominational leaders, and executives in Christian organizations all over the U.S. and Canada who are in the same plight. Some are getting nowhere. Quite a few are working their way out because of attention to a few basic management principles.

This chapter deals with the most basic of these: *setting and working against clear objectives.*

But before we talk about this basic principle, let's first look at Christian organizations and why they are prone to various forms of down-in-the-mud disease.

Christian Organizations Are Different

Christian organizations *are* different—or at least they should be! They are different because they have a higher allegiance than the basic purpose of the organization. They work on the assumption that they are doing something, are part of something, that has an eternal value.

15

They are different because the individuals in the organization share in this common allegiance to a "God who is there." And because they have this higher and common purpose, they assume a moral and ethical level which should always transcend their short-term goals.

This means that they must continually place a high value on the individual and his personal development and needs. That's an easy statement to make, but in practice it takes on tremendous implications. When do we put the good of the organization above the immediate needs of the individual? How far can we go in letting the desperate plight of one member divert the group from its calling?

Most Christian organizations have a degree of volunteerism to them. At one end of the scale is the organization that pays all its members a salary, but makes special demands on them because of this higher allegiance. At the other end is the local church, with very few, if any, paid workers. In this respect the local church is one of the most complicated and sophisticated kinds of organizations in the world. It's one thing to lead a group of people who are dependent on the organization for their livelihood. It's quite another to motivate a group 99 percent of whom are volunteers!

Fortunately, we are slowly learning that the *best* management methods work in both extremes. (We'll discuss this in a later chapter.)

What's Wrong with the Bogged Down Organizations?

Regardless of the many different kinds of symptoms, the basic problem is usually the absence of clearly defined, highly communicable objectives.

The organization may have a grand purpose ("witness to Christ," "serve mankind," "care for the needy"), but too often that purpose is not stated in terms of what we intend to *do* to accomplish that purpose. One of the major signs of this malady is a large number of committees, departments, or boards that are organized around *what* they do rather than what task they are trying to complete. In the local church this might show itself in a multiplying number of boards of Christian education, visitation committees, ushering committees, building committees, etc. When these groups are formed, they usually have a clear idea of why and what. But after ten years, their original goals become fuzzy and institutional hardening of the arteries sets in. Each year new budgets are approved which are just an extension of "What we did last year, plus . . ."

Staff is added to carry out this function or that. People are asked to "serve on this committee for three years." People are recruited less and less on the value of what is to be accomplished and more and more on allegiance to the organization. ("After all, this is *our* church. . . .") Sound familiar?

How Do You Get Moving Again?

Start with yourself. Do you, as a Christian leader, have a clear picture of what you want to *do* and *be* in one year, five years, at the end of your lifetime? Write down in action-oriented, measurable terms your goals for *you*. You can't lead other people in defining their goals if you don't know your own.

State your idea of the basic purpose of your organization and then write some five-year goals for it. Five years from now how is your world going to be different because of what you and your organization have done? How will you (and the rest of the world) know this has happened?

Now consider what kind of an organization and what kinds of people are needed to accomplish these tasks.

Wherever possible make all organization groupings around tasks, *not* functions.

Set dates for when each task and sub-task is to be completed, and plan to disband the task force when it has reached its goals.

But What about Others?

This all sounds very good in theory. In practice it's not easy at all. In fact it's much easier to keep on fighting fires and have committee meetings that seem to get nowhere.

People are uneasy with the lack of results, but many people like change even less. It's not easy to switch from "this-is-how-we-do-it-here" thinking to "this-is-what-we-want-to-get-done."

Here are a few basic steps to establishing organizational goals which will capture the allegiance of your group.

1. *Bring together key people* who can lead others. Ask them to start dreaming and thinking with you about what your organization should have accomplished in five years.
2. *Bring in other people* early in the process. Perhaps an organization planning retreat by departments or other groups. Remember the principle of goal ownership: "Good goals are my goals, and bad goals are your goals."
3. *Prioritize the many good ideas* you'll get and decide on a few over-arching purposes and some specific major goals for each year.
4. *Analyze what steps* would be needed to accomplish these goals.
5. *Estimate the cost* in people, dollars, and facilities.
6. *Assign specific people to the task.*
7. *Communicate your goals* in every way possible. Preach them, measure them, talk about them!

8. *Remember you are in a process.* Each year the situation will change. New goals will have to be set.

Make a typed copy and run it through your copy machine. Use it for a worksheet in doing your own personal planning.

Operational Goals

A goal can be a very beautiful statement of what you hope will happen someday, but it is no more useful than the plans, people, and resources that will be needed to make it happen.

On page 21 we have given you a worksheet that you can use to make sure your goals are operational. What we mean by "operational" will come out in the description that follows.

Every goal should have a **purpose.** State your reasons first for *why* you want to do something. Now state the **goal.** What is it you plan to accomplish? But note that the difference between a goal and a purpose is that a goal is *measurable*. Therefore, you need to have a date by which the goal will be accomplished or you will have begun the program that you want to institute. But you will also need to know how you are going to measure whether or not you actually met the goal. How will we know that it happened? This measurement may be in the form of indicators, such as number of people who are involved, or in the case of something more definitive, like the building of a new building. The very fact of its existence will be a measurement.

A goal is no better than the plan to accomplish it. We will discuss planning in the following chapters. Suffice it to say here that we need to describe the **steps** that will lead us to the goal.

But who will be responsible? Who will be the **people** who

are going to "own" these goals? If nobody owns them, chances are very high that they will never be accomplished.

Do you have the resources? What will it **cost?** Cost obviously cannot be calculated until you have decided on the steps you are going to take to reach the goal. Therefore you may go through the entire process only to discover that you can't afford to accomplish the goal! Don't be discouraged. You now know another way that won't work! Copy off the worksheet (Figure 1) and use it to lead people through this discussion. You will perhaps need a much larger piece of paper, but just taking people through the logic will be a big step.

Books That Can Help

For the serious beginner, Charles Hughes' *Goal Setting* (American Management Association) is a very readable discussion of the entire process, from a secular view.

Goal Analysis by Robert Mager (Fearon Press) is a delightful book that will help you to ascertain the difference between a purpose and a goal. It is available in paper.

Two books by Lyle Schaller, both in paperback, and both published by Abingdon, are closer to where most Christian executives and pastors live. *Parish Planning* is just what the title implies, with a lot of good basic material. *The Change Agent* deals with the problem from the view of the person trying to work from within the organization.

Ed Dayton's workbook *God's Purpose/Man's Plans* is available from MARC, 919 W. Huntington Drive, Monrovia, CA 91016. It covers goals, planning and problem solving from a Christian perspective.

If you are new to the entire business of leading a Christian organization, try Engstrom and Mackenzie's *Managing Your Time.* Zondervan has it in paperback.

Get Started! You can't change direction unless you're moving.

OPERATIONAL GOAL FOR: _____
                       Name of the program

PURPOSE For this reason: _____

                           _____

                           _____

                           _____

GOAL   We plan to
         accomplish
         this: _____

                           _____

                           _____

                           _____

         by this date: _____

         We will know
         that it hap-
         pened because: _____

                           _____

STEPS   We plan to
         take these
         steps: _____

                           _____

                           _____

                           _____

PEOPLE: These people
         are responsible: _____

                           _____

COST   It will cost
         this amount: _____

                           _____

                           _____

Figure 1

2.

Christian Leadership— What Is It?

Leadership can be looked at from many different angles.

Leadership is a *position*. Companies have leaders. Organizations have leaders. Groups have leaders.

Leadership is a *relationship*. Leaders are persons who have followers—by definition. People may follow because of inspiration, self-interest, or because of organizational structures, but followers there must be.

Leadership is *actions*. Leaders are known by the leadership acts they perform. A person may have a long list of the attributes or traits of a leader, but if he never takes leadership action, he is not (yet) a leader.

Christian leadership differs from other forms of leadership basically in its motivation, the "why?" of its actions.

How to Define a Leader?

For years there has been a running argument about how to define a leader. Is he a leader because of the qualities or attributes he brings to the role? Is he a leader as a result of his relationship to a group? Is he a leader because of the things that he does?

There has been a general confusion between the person or role of the leader and that of the manager (or administrator or executive or director or general or ruler or whatever name the position carries). This confusion is quite natural. Persons who turn out to be good leaders find themselves in positions of leadership. Since they are seldom identified as leaders until the time they assume the leadership role, it is difficult to distinguish between the man and the role.

"Leadership is of utmost importance. Indeed, there is no substitute for it. But leadership cannot be created or promoted. It cannot be taught or learned." So wrote the dean of management experts, Peter Drucker, in *The Practice of Management* (Harper & Row, 1954, p. 158). Drucker believes that the task of the organization is to create the conditions under which potential leadership qualities become effective.

To put it another way, leadership qualities are part of the basic makeup of the individual. They will not necessarily become evident until that individual is found in a leadership situation. Most, if not all, the men and women who are found in leadership positions have been put there because their leadership ability has been recognized. If you or your associates do not have the basic makeup of a leader, you will not become one. But it does not follow that men and women who are potential leaders will automatically find leadership roles.

Are There Basic Qualities?

Are there, then, basic qualities that all leaders will have to some measure? Observers of leaders, and men who have been leaders themselves, seem to point to a handful of attributes that seem to be universal. Some of these attributes are either genetic or are closely wrapped up in the social environment. Others are acquired.

① *Selfless dedication* is how General Eisenhower describes

the first one ("What Is Leadership," *Reader's Digest*, June, 1965, p. 50). There is about a leader a belief in what he is doing, the goal he is trying to reach, the cause he espouses, that transcends himself. He is willing to sacrifice even himself to accomplish the task.

②This takes *courage*. To hold on in spite of the apparent obstacles, to make a decision with inadequate information, to risk reputation and material well-being, require a courage based on conviction.

A major portion of this courage will demonstrate itself ③ in *decisiveness*. Decisions must be made. Other men vacillate. The leader makes a decision and moves ahead.

④   Leadership requires *persuasiveness*. If men and women are to follow, they must be convinced that the goals and aspirations of the leader are worthy of their dedication and be motivated to attempt them.

Interestingly, there is almost universal agreement that ⑤ the most outstanding leaders have had a *humility* which has resulted in their accepting responsibility for failure as well as success.

Up to this point we have been describing qualities which might be held by almost anyone in any walk of life. But for the vast majority of leadership situations there must be ⑥ *competence*, the individual must have skills in the area in which he is working. Without competence few wars will be won, no ocean liner will dock, no organization (Christian or other) will long survive. Competence, of course, assumes intelligence and creativity to whatever degree required.

Many people think of leaders as having a great deal of personality. Both personal observation and a small amount of research will quickly show you that "personality" is *not* one of the basic qualities. There are leaders who are personally warm and affable. There are others who are cold and aloof.

Nor can leaders be typed by the way in which they go about their task. There are many different styles of leadership—dictatorial, autocratic, benevolent, democratic. Some men lead by example. Others lead by sensing the direction of the crowd. Some are problem solvers who work well in groups. Others may pride themselves on their decision-making ability and rejoice in the personal quick decision. In the complex societies in which most of us work, men who hold positions of leadership in dynamic organizations have learned to adopt their style to the situation.

How to Find Good Leaders

But if Drucker is right, if leadership "cannot be taught or learned," what can we do to find, equip, and select the best leaders? The answer lies in building organizations which encourage and promote these basic qualities. Leadership *is* situational. It is a combination of the right leader leading the right group in the right set of circumstances. (The most competent leader is the one who can continue to exercise leadership in the broadest number of situations.) Do you want to attract and nurture good leaders? Build into your organization goals and objectives that require dedication and courage. Set high standards of conduct, responsibility, and performance. Demonstrate respect for the individual and his work. Create a climate where good leaders will be recognized and nurtured.

Once such a climate exists, good leaders will begin to identify themselves. It is at this point that training can begin. As we said earlier, a leader must have adequate competence in his field. If a man or woman is to assume broader responsibilities, he must have the specific training needed. This can be obtained formally by more academic work or on-the-job. If on-the-job, then care should be taken that both he and his supervisor understand the (measurable) objectives of his training.

It does not follow that because a man is technically outstanding that he is necessarily a leader. Putting a technically competent person in a leadership position when he is not a leader may only serve to prove the Peter Principle. ("All men eventually rise to the level of their incompetency.")

Are There Leadership Capability Tests?

Yes, there are. Enough has been learned by now to predict with reasonable accuracy whether an adult is a potential leader. Your local university, state employment service, or private testing agency may all be able to help.

What Is Christian Leadership?

So far we have said very little about *Christian* leadership other than to note that it differs basically in its motivation. However, it has been of continuing interest to us that those organizations which place a high priority on the worth of the individual, on high standards of personal conduct, on good communication, both up and down, organizations which have righteous convictions, out-perform the others. It has also been our observation that too often Christian organizations have had lower standards of individual and corporate performances than secular ones.

What is *Christian* leadership? It is leadership motivated by love and given over to service. It is leadership that has been subjected to the control of Christ and his example. The best Christian leaders exemplify to the utmost all those attributes of selfless dedication, courage, decisiveness, compassion, and persuasiveness that mark the great leader.

The truly Christian leader has discovered that leadership

begins with the towel and the basin—in the role of a servant.

Selfless dedication is possible because the Christian knows that God has a grand strategy of which he is a part.

Courage is magnified by the power that comes through the indwelling Spirit.

Decisiveness comes from knowing that ultimate responsibility does not lie with him.

Persuasiveness is based on allegiance to a cause that transcends all causes.

Compassion is the human expression of Christ's concern for the individual.

Humility results from knowing that it is God who does the work.

Are You a Leader?

Are you a Christian leader? Lead! The *purpose* of leadership is to lead.

Books You Might Want to Read

Ted Engstrom's *The Making of a Christian Leader* (Zondervan, 1976) enlarges greatly on what we have been saying here.

Man at the Top by Richard Wolff (Tyndale, 1969) is the only book we know that attempts a look at leadership from a Christian perspective. Worth having.

The Effective Executive is Peter Drucker's work directed at the individual organizational leader. Available from Harper & Row (1966).

For a discussion on the environment that might permit good leaders to flourish, see *The Human Organization* by Rensis Likert (McGraw-Hill, 1967).

3.

Leadership Style

What is leadership? No one seems to be really sure. We are able to define what *managers* do, but the closest we seem to be able to come to a broadly acceptable definition of leadership is, that which leaders do. Then when we try to define leader, about all the agreement we could get is that leaders lead.

Leadership As a Style

Perhaps in despair over defining leadership, management theorists have attempted to picture it in terms of *style*. In using such a broad term they are attempting to describe how the person operates, rather than what he is. If you think about a number of leaders that you know personally, you can probably come up with your own summation of their style: "He's a player/coach kind of guy," or "she's a prima donna," or "he's a one man show." In other words, we tend to characterize a leader on the way he leads by our personal perception of him or her. It follows that one person may feel differently than another about a leader's style. "Style" turns out to be the summation of how the leader goes about carrying out his leadership function and how he is perceived by those he is attempting to lead or those who may be observing from the sidelines.

What Leadership Styles Are There?

Since leadership style includes how a person operates within the context of his organization, it is easiest to discuss different kinds of style by describing the type of organization or situation which either results from or is appropriate for a particular style. Our concern of the moment is with those who are in positions of leadership already, rather than those who are wondering about their potential skills. We will discuss five leadership styles: Bureaucratic, permissive, laissez-faire, participative, and autocratic. We will look at each one of these in terms of how the leader operates *within the organization*.

1- Bureaucratic—This is a style marked by a continual reference to organization rules and regulations. It is assumed that somehow difficulties can be ironed out if everyone will abide by the rules. Decisions are made by parliamentary procedures. The leader is a diplomat and learns how to use the majority rule as a way to get people to perform. Compromise is a way of life because in order to have one decision accepted by the majority it is often necessary to give in on another one.

2- Permissive—Here the desire is to keep everyone in the group satisfied. Keeping people happy is the name of the game. It is assumed that if people feel good about themselves and others that the organization will function, and thus the job will get done. Coordination often suffers with this style.

3- Laissez-faire—This is practically no leadership at all and allows everything to run its own course. The leader simply performs a maintenance function. For example, a pastor may act as a figurehead as far as the leadership of the organization is concerned and concern himself only with his preaching while others are left to work out the details of how the organization should operate. This style is sometimes used by leaders who are away a great deal or who have been temporarily put in charge.

✔-Participative—This is used by those who believe the way to motivate others is to involve them in the decision-making process. This hopefully creates goal ownership and a feeling of shared purpose. Here the problem is the delay in action in times of crisis.

5- Autocratic—This is marked by reliance upon authority and usually assumes that people will not do anything unless told to. It discourages innovation. The leader sees himself as indispensable. Decisions can be made quickly.

What Do These Styles Assume?

Notice that each one of these styles depends to a large extent on one's view of people and what motivates them. Since the function of leadership is to lead, getting people to follow is of primary importance. *The Bureaucratic leader* somehow believes that everyone can agree on the best way to do things and that there is some system outside of human relationships that can be used as a guide. Hence rules and regulations.

The permissive leader wants everyone (including himself) to feel good. Internal stress is viewed as being bad for the organization (and perhaps even unchristian).

The laissez-faire leader either assumes that the organization is running so well that he can't add to it, or he assumes that organizations really don't need a focal point of leadership.

The participative leader usually enjoys solving problems and working with others. He assumes that others feel the same way, and therefore, the most will be accomplished by working together and sharing all decisions and goals.

The autocratic leader assumes that people will only do what they are told to do and/or that he knows what is best. In other words, he may appear to be a dictator. (But he can also be a benevolent dictator.)

Which Style Is Best?

Leaders are different. But so are followers! Which is another way of saying that some situations demand one style of leader, while others demand a different one. Leaders are different. At any given time the leadership needs of an organization may vary from another time. Since organizations have difficulty continually changing their leaders, it follows that those leaders will need *different styles* at *different times.* The appropriate style depends a great deal on the task of the organization, the phase of life of the organization, and the needs of the moment.

What might be some examples of how the *task of the organization* affects leadership style? A fire department cannot perform without at least some autocratic leadership. When the time comes for the organization to perform, to do what it was designed to do, autocratic leadership is a must. There is no time to sit down and discuss how to attack the fire. One trained person has to decide for the group, and the group must abide by his decision. Later on there may be a more free discussion on which way will be best next time. On the other hand, a medical group might best be operated with a permissive style.

An autocratic style may even be needed in a Christian organization! In times of crisis, such as the evacuation of mission personnel, or the need to radically reduce costs, the leader often must act unilaterally.

Organizations go through different *phases in their life.*

During periods of rapid growth and expansion, autocratic leadership may work very well. For example, the founder of a new Christian organization, or the founding pastor of a church, is often a charismatic figure who knows intuitively what is to be done and how to do it. Since the vision is his, he is best able to impart it to others without discussion. But during periods of slow growth or consolidation, the organization needs to be much more reflective to attempt to be more efficient. Participative leadership may be the order of the day.

Both of these considerations need to be tempered by the *needs of the moment*. Using autocratic leadership may work well for fire fighting (either real or figurative), but it will probably be less than successful in dealing with a personal problem. An emergency in the medical group may demand that someone assume (autocratic) leadership.

Fitting Style to Organization

It follows that ideally a leader should have many different styles. He should be a man for all seasons, shifting from the permissiveness of summer to the demands of winter.

Looking at it from the side of the organization, the organization needs to adopt a *strategy for effectiveness*, taking into account its needs and its "product." Most voluntary organizations and not-for-profit organizations are founded on the assumption of a common vision and shared goals. They have a strategy of *seeking success* (reaching their goals). When the organization is young, the founder can depend on his strength of vision to attract others who share his goals. However, as the organization is successful other means of maintaining a common vision will be needed. If the leadership style is not modified to include participative sharing of goals, too often the organization will adopt the strategy of *avoiding failure*. When the organization reaches a size where an autocratic style will no longer work if the leader is unable to switch to a participative style, many times he is forced (and perhaps unknowingly) to adopt a laissez-faire style. Meanwhile the second level of leadership (which is now forced to run the organization) is most likely to adopt a bureaucratic style.

Where Are You?

What is your leadership style? A cursory examination of some of the management literature will help you discover that. Hopefully you will discover that you have exercised different types of leadership style at different times. Do you have evidence that you *can* change your style as needed? Or, as you think of the decisions that have been made in the past six months do you discover that they were always made the same way (by you, by others, together, or by the bureaucracy)?

Where Is Your Organization?

What kind of leadership does your organization need at this time? What is its task? What phase of organizational growth are you in? What are different needs of this moment? Analyze this with help from your board, leadership team, members, etc. Are different styles of leadership needed for different areas of organizational life?

Where Do You Go from Here?

Review your calendar of meetings for the past two weeks. What happened in those meetings? Did you go to meetings just to announce your own decision (autocratic style)? Did you go to the meeting expecting to work with the group to arrive at a decision (participative style)? Did you go expecting to sit back and let others worry about the problem (permissive style)? Or, did you go intending to use the parliamentary procedures to make sure that the ship stayed on an even keel (bureaucratic style)? Perhaps you didn't go at all (laissez-faire)!

If you discovered that you handled each meeting in the same way, you are probably locked into one style and should consider knowingly setting about to attempt to modify your style as a function of the situation which you are in. By deciding before the meeting the style you will adopt you will give yourself the advantage of being able to observe the response of the other members of the meeting.

If you have been limiting yourself to one style, sudden changes will often result in confusion in others. It may be necessary for you to very clearly spell out the ground rules as to how you are anticipating the decision-making process will work.

For Additional Reading

Management Styles in Transition by Glenn A. Basset (American Management Association) analyzes leadership style and strategy along with leadership skill and competence within the context of changing needs within organizations and a good analysis of how organizations work.

4.

A Christian Philosophy
of Management

I (Ed Dayton) recently had a letter asking my views on a Christian philosophy of management. I really worked this one over. What was it about my being a Christian that impacted on my management philosophy? As a student of management, an active manager in a large Christian service agency, and a teacher and resource person in management seminars, I obviously should have an answer. And I find I do. But the trouble is most people will think it is the wrong answer. For I don't think there *is* a Christian philosophy of management any more than I think there is a Christian philosophy of bus driving! To me the question reflects an attempt to divide the secular and the sacred. They refuse to be divided.

David Secunda, who is vice president of the American Management Association and a thoughtful Christian, sums it up this way in a recent letter:

> Management, as I see it, contains nothing that is incompatible with Christian principle or belief. It is a means to an end—not an end unto itself— and does not presume an agreement on ends. At its core is the effort to enhance the human po-

tential and without this, it becomes a box of tools and techniques, useful but also subject to good intelligent misuse. Likewise there is no excuse to justify the bad or ill-managed Christian organization. Believers have no more license to be ineffective when dealing with human resources than does a surgeon. Lives are at stake in both cases.

But, management as a process can benefit from change or an additional dimension. One such is a sounder being that would emerge from a blending of management and Christian fundamentals. We have not done this but there is no reason why you shouldn't try. However, it can't be done from books and computers, even though they have a place. The understanding of each alone takes much of a man—to do both demands unusual commitment but the prize may be worth the try.

Our Failure Is Practice, Not Philosophy

Now, there no doubt are men in management positions (both secular and Christian) who are operating in very unchristian ways. They are using their position to manipulate for their personal gain; they are conducting their business in ways that violate accepted ethics or perhaps even the laws of the land. They may be dealing with other human beings in very unloving ways. But as I read most current management theory, it seems very Christian indeed! There is increasing awareness that helping an individual grow as a person within the context of the organization's goal is good for the organization and good for the individual. Like good bus driving, the *rules* of a well-played game are reasonably obvious. The failure is not in the philosophy, or lack thereof, but in the practice. Again we are reminded that it is not things that are sinful, but men!

We Would Like It Black and White

Before attending seminary at age forty, I spent seventeen years in industry, most of the time with two well-known aerospace corporations. As an aware Christian I kept looking for black-and-white situations against which to measure my involvement with my company. Most of the time it was mushy grey. The standard practice manuals of those two companies were beyond reproach. Their established business practices were in complete line with what I considered to be biblical ethics. In many ways they appeared to recognize that they were dealing with sin-prone people, both within and without their organization. Only twice in seventeen years did I have occasion to challenge as wrong a company procedure or activity. In both cases the company immediately corrected the situation.

In the midst of these highly ethical organizations I found myself among sinful men, including myself. Some were blatantly so. They intended to get "ahead in the world," and they didn't seem to care who knew it. Others were men of goodwill who fell prey to their own desires.

Christian Organizations Are Even Greyer

During the last nine years I have been through three years at a topflight seminary and have been on the management staff of a large evangelical Christian service organization. During this time I have had the opportunity to be involved with a good number of Christian organizations from local churches to denominational headquarters, from overseas mission staffs to mission organizations within the United States. The black-and-white picture that I hoped would emerge as I moved from the "secular" to the "Christian" world has just not come into focus. In fact, if anything, I would have to say that the situation within the world in which I now live and work is even a mushier grey than it was before.

Why Is This So?

Why is this so? Why should my experience be that I have found many Christian organizations who act in much less Christian manner than some of their secular counterparts? I have thought about this a great deal, and I would offer the following suggestions.

Most Christian organizations do not have the luxury of clear-cut measures of performance. The profit-making company must make a profit in order to stay in business. It may have other more altruistic goals than just making a profit. But without that profit it cannot exist. Most Christian organizations, on the other hand, find it very difficult to set up standards of measurement against which they can audit their own performance.

Christian organizations usually assume a common allegiance to a higher purpose. Because this is so they have few checks and balances in asking their employees to put out more work, whether it be in the form of overtime, extra responsibility, or sacrificing family for the organization. It would be my belief here that they are operating in a very unbiblical manner, because of my strong conviction that the Bible puts our commitment to one another above the work to which we are called. The other side of this coin is the fact that many of the employees, who are usually working for a wage considerably less than the standard outside, feel that they are part owners of the organization and as such have a right to question anything that goes on or instructions that they receive.

"This is the Lord's work . . ." is used in a number of

other ways. I am sure that most of what is done is quite subconscious, but too often we excuse poor working conditions, low pay, poor quality, or generally substandard personnel relations on the basis that we are conserving the Lord's money.

"We are all Christians here . . ." is used as an excuse for not having thought out procedures, particularly personnel procedures. Too often the assumption is made that being a Christian automatically gives one a common ethical base on which to work. As a result we can easily slip into business practices which are less than ethical.

What Can We Do to Improve?

If, as has been my personal observation, Christian organizations. come out second-best when measured against secular organizations, what is the answer? As a Christian, what should be my philosophy of management? Just good management.

Excellence

It would always begin with excellence. If it is "the Lord's work," and it *is* worth doing, then it is worth doing with *excellence*. Every standard we set should be set as high as we can possibly set it.

Purpose

We then need a clearly defined *purpose* which is undergirded by a set of equally clear goals, goals which are both measurable and accomplishable. These purposes and goals should be used as the basis of the people we hire, the procedures we write, the facilities we acquire, the programs we carry out.

Communicated Goals

Christians should communicate. If we *are* the body of

Christ, let's have the nervous system working. <u>Goals should be clearly communicated to all those who are responsible for them.</u> Here we enter the whole area of management by objective, the common building and sharing of goals. There is a need for goals to flow up from the bottom and to come down from the top. There is a need to identify and creatively resolve conflicts between management and subordinate goals, not necessarily to the mutual satisfaction of all concerned, but certainly with the mutual understanding of all concerned.

Goals center our thinking on the *task*, and keep us from becoming functionally obsolescent. There is nothing worse than an organization that has become so wrapped up in its function that it has lost sight of its purpose. Goals are like a suspension bridge that at one end rests on purpose, and on the other rests on function. They make certain that there is an open road between the two. The moment we discover that our *Christian* organization has become more interested in self-perpetuation than accomplishing a purpose, that's the time to push the **self-destruct** button. (And that takes courage!)

The Needs of People

Finally, I would continually struggle with the needs of people. In every organization that attempts to concern itself with its own people, there will always be a tension between caring for the individual and reaching the goals of the organization. It is in this area that we probably have more biblical guidelines than in any other area of management. A Christian view of management must include a constant review of the needs of the individuals involved. There will be many times where the desires, or even the personal welfare, of the individual may have to be subordinated to the good of the group or the achievement of the task. But let's make certain we spend enough time to recognize the particular conflict and the implications of its resolution.

A Christian philosophy of management? Perhaps. More appropriately, let's have a Christian view of *life*.

5.

Planning—Part One

It is not a question of whether we will make plans or not. Not to plan is a plan in itself, for planning is basically nothing more than attempting to decide in advance what we will or will not do in the next minutes, hours, days, months or years. For the Christian leader, planning asks the question as to whether we will affect the future at random or with purpose. Because affect it we will. We have a responsibility to decide what we should be or do, and therefore *must* plan.

Planning Has a Poor Track Record

In his very readable book, *The Human Side of Planning* (published by Macmillan, 1969), David Ewing points out that in general planning has a poor track record. He's right. Ewing believes that a major difficulty has been the failure of planners to take into account and into their confidence the people for whom they are planning. But there is another side of the story. Many people's understanding of planning is narrow and confining. They picture plans as two high walls between which they must walk. Some Christians see such predetermined decision as actually presumptuous and an affront to God.

Planning Starts with Goals

<u>Planning must be based on measurable, accomplishable</u> goals.

It has been well said, "If you don't care where you're going, any road will take you there." It's not always easy to clearly define what it is we want to be or do, but the failure of many plans can be laid at the door of fuzzy goals. Communication is a difficult business at best, and if our goals are not clear and communicable, they will not attract clear and communicable plans.

Planning Is Trying to Write Future History

Man is a future-oriented being. He plans on the basis of what he has perceived in the past, but he tries to project this understanding into the future. Except for the most simple, close-in projects, it is very unlikely that our predictions about the future will be 100 percent accurate. The old adage "If something can go wrong, it probably will" is another way of saying that there are so many more possibilities that something other than what we expected and hoped for will happen, that the probability of things happening *our* way is remote.

From a Christian viewpoint most of life is failure! "A miss is as good as a mile." 99 percent is sin (failure). But we have learned that we live in an imperfect world. The unexpected and the unpredictable keep throwing us off balance. Planning attempts to wipe some of the mist away from the window of the future and reduce the number and the impact of the surprises.

Planning is therefore an attempt to move from "now" to "then," to change things from the way "things are" to the way "things ought to be."

Planning Is an Arrow

Since no man can be sure of the future, why plan? Basically to improve the probability that what we believe should happen will happen. The goal has been staked out in the future of our minds: "to reach that fire lookout tower on the top of that mountain by tomorrow noon," "to provide adequate funds so that our children can go to college," "to begin a new ministry in a ghetto area," "to install a new training program for our organization." You name it. The point of the planning arrow figuratively touches the goal. The steps that need to be accomplished stretch back along the arrow into the present to create a "plan."

Planning Is a Process

If plans are considered as fixed and unchangeable, then most likely they will fail. Planning is a *process*. The necessary steps are laid out, pointing toward the future goal, but as each major step is taken, a reevaluation, or feedback, process that calls us first to reexamine the future at each step and secondly measures the extent of our progress. If we have set a goal to have a hundred new members in our church during the next twelve months, we had better not wait until the eleventh month to see how we are doing. If we are planning to drive 1,000 miles across unfamiliar territory, it is best to look at the road map once in a while and measure progress. If we plan to train a group for a new assignment and put them to work in six months, check points along the way will be needed.

And yet time and time again we fail to evaluate progress. And sometimes we even set up an evaluation program and then fail to use it. Why? Many times it's because the measurement may take as much energy as the program itself. Other times, we are so wrapped up in what we are doing that we just forget (or don't want) to ask, "How are we doing?"

Planning Takes Time

But it's worth every minute. But most of us won't take the time unless we consciously set it aside. A daily time to make up things-to-do list should be a regular habit. Setting times of monthly, quarterly, and yearly review on our calendars will build the process into the regular "work" we need to do each day.

And because planning takes time it should be begun as far in advance as possible. For example, in a church don't wait until October to start planning for the next year! The process should begin no later than April or May so that as many people as possible can be brought in and so you are not rushed into the future.

The evaluation process should therefore be just as much a part of our planning as reaching the steps to reaching the goal. Someone should be made responsible for the measurement, usually (not the person responsible for the achievement.

Planning Is Both Personal and Corporate

Don't be misled into believing that planning for tomorrow is useful only for groups. Goal setting and planning must become a personal style of life if they are to be truly effective. There is a direct relationship between a man's effectiveness in his personal life and his effectiveness in his organizational life.

Applying the planning process to the family and interpersonal relationships will sharpen one's overall understanding of where he fits and how he is relating to those around him.

Planning Is People

Or it should be! To go back to Ewing's observation, to omit the people part of the planning equation is to court disaster. In the next chapter we will give some techniques for involving people in the planning process. Suffice it to point out here that whenever possible plans should, to the greatest extent, be made by the people who are going to do the work. For example, the task of a planning committee should not be to plan for other people, but rather to give them the information they need on which to base their plans ("What will our community be like in ten years?") and to give training, counsel, and/or coordination in planning.

Plans Communicate Our Intentions

As the population of the world grows, and our means of communicating with one another grow more sophisticated, the *opportunities* for working together grow at an ever-increasing rate. In the Western world the number of different roles we play as individuals (father, husband, friend, churchman, club member, driver, etc.) and as members of organizations (ministry, employee care, social responsibility, legal restrictions, etc.) grow at a fantastic rate. The number of "intersections" with other people's plans grows accordingly. It is as though the world had become completely overlaid with side streets, highways, and expressways, each one of them representing someone's (or some organization's) plans. If we are not clear in deciding where we are going and how we (presently) plan to get there, we will find ourselves continually colliding with other people's plans.

In a local church it may be the failure of the choir director to communicate his plans for a big children's festival at a time when the Sunday school was hoping to involve the same children in a new venture. In a larger organization "collisions" may occur because one department has not adequately conveyed its intentions to use space, machine time, or manpower. In an even larger context, time and time again one organization moves ahead with plans without ascertaining the intentions of other organizations or sharing their own plans. The result is not only overlap and duplication, but great confusion among those whom these different organizations are attempting to serve.

By announcing our goals and clearly indicating the steps we currently plan to take to achieve them, we establish intersection points with others who are also making new plans and working on old ones.

Steps in Plans Are Sub-Goals

Once all the alternative approaches have been analyzed, put aside, and final plans laid, it is useful to remember that each step of the plan is actually a goal in itself. Each step should therefore have the same characteristics as the end goal of the project: it should be accomplishable and measurable. It should also have a date and the name of the person responsible. Regardless of what method of planning is used (and there are many), failure to assign dates and responsible individuals to each step of the plan will lessen the probability of success.

"Fail to plan, plan to fail." It's that simple.

For Further Reading

We have already mentioned David Ewing's *The Human*

Side of Planning. Lyle Schaller's *The Change Agent* will be helpful here, as well as Ed Dayton's *God's Purpose/ Man's Plans.*

6.

Planning—Part Two

Start with the Goal

The first step for any successful planning effort begins with clearly defined and communicable goals. It cannot be said too often: fuzzy goals will produce fuzzy plans. So start with your goals. Make certain that all the persons involved are as much a part of the goal setting process as possible.

Gather Ideas

Sometimes, once a goal has been set, the steps needed to reach that goal—plans—are immediately apparent. But often we need to gather as many ideas as possible before going further. If these suggestions can come forth from the group that is going to carry on the work, so much the better.

One effective brainstorming technique for gathering ideas from a group is the slip technique. Give each person in the group a supply of paper slips (about 3-by-5 inches). A group of four to eight persons seated around a table is an optimum size. If you have a larger group, you might want to subdivide it. Then, *having clearly stated the goal,* and written it on a slip of paper, start asking questions that will produce ideas: "What has to happen before we reach this goal?" "What else has to happen?" "What has to happen before *that?*" As each person responds, give only one reply, "Good! Write that down." The individual giving the suggestion writes his own suggestion on a slip of paper, one slip for each idea. (Ask them to print. You'll want to be able to read them later!) It also helps if the leader repeats what has been suggested. Try to always include a verb in the statement: not "agenda," but "agenda planned."

You will discover that a group that is at all familiar with the problem at hand will produce a large number of suggestions in a very short time. Be careful not to evaluate or judge any suggestion. That will come later.

If the group seems momentarily stalled, pick up one of the previous slips, read it and ask, "What has to happen before *that?*"

The advantage of using individually written slips over a chalkboard or a secretary is, first, the rapidity with which ideas can be gathered, second, the participation of as many people as possible, third, and most important, the fact that the ideas can be rearranged later on. The technique is effective even if you are working by yourself.

Sort Out the Steps

Once you have gathered as many ideas as you can, first lay out the slips on a table or tack them on a corkboard. Rearrange them from left to right in time sequence. Which need to be done first? Which are dependent on others? You will discover that some ideas just don't fit. They can be set aside. Some ideas will conflict with one another. Here you will have to decide which way to go. But the

Use individual slips for brainstorming
1. Rapid
2. Greater participation
3. Can rearrange ideas later

very fact that everyone's ideas have been considered will ease the task.

While you are doing this, you will no doubt discover other steps that are needed. "Good, write that down."

Establish Dates

Once all the major steps needed to reach the goal have been agreed upon, estimate the time each event will take. On the basis of this estimate put a date down when each step must begin and when it must end. You may discover at this point that you don't have enough time to reach the goal. Replan. Find new ways that will do it. More manpower. More resources. Drop out lower priority steps.

Assign Personnel

No step of any plan will happen unless someone knows and accepts his responsibility for the step. Put a name (s) on each slip. Each step should be viewed as a sub-goal to the overall goal. And each one needs to be "owned" by someone.

Design an Evaluation System

Decide on evaluation points along the way. The number of such points will depend on the length of the total program. There probably needs to be more in the second half of the project.

Checkpoints can be committee meetings, a checkup phone call from a group leader, a written report. But make sure they are established just as firmly as the other events in your plan. You can play the same game again, only this time ask the question, "How can we be sure this step is taken?"

Organize and Display Your Plans

It is important that everyone involved has all the understanding and information about the total plan that they need. On pages 57, 58 we have given two forms of organizing and presenting plans.

Figure 2 is a form of checklist that can be used to describe the event, note the names of people involved, and the beginning and ending dates. Information from the slip technique can be transferred to this list, or if you wish you can start with the form itself. Note that once such a sheet has been filled out it becomes a checklist for the next time the same task is carried out (or modified as the new situation may dictate).

Figure 3 is a bar chart or Gantt chart. (Don't be disturbed by the name!) Notice that it has the ability to break the plan up into different groupings. The bar represents the total time for that phase. The diamonds along the bar represent steps (from your slips) that have to do with this phase. This is a very compact display whose major advantage is that it shows the relationship of many different events. This is a big advantage when a number of individuals are involved.

The advantage of both these planning charts is that they pack a great deal of information into a small area and thus strengthen communication.

Work Your Plan

Don't let it work you. Take a major step and evaluate. There's no disgrace in changing a plan. Tomorrow will always present new problems and new opportunities.

PROJECT LIST

ITEM NO.	DESCRIPTION	BROWN	JONES	SMITH	WHITE	AVIS	SCHEDULE Begin	SCHEDULE Complete
		RESPONSIBLE PERSON						
1	POSSIBLE SPEAKERS	X				X	1-7-72	1-11-72
2	PROGRAM OUTLINE		X				1-15-72	1-22-72
3	SELECT SITE			X			1-18-72	1-22-72
4	TENTATIVE BUDGET				X		1-7-72	1-8-72
5	SPEAKERS CONTACTED	X	X				1-11-72	1-20-72
6	PROGRAM NOTES		X			X	1-22-72	2-5-72
7	FACILITY CONTRACT			X			1-30-72	2-10-72

Figure 2

PLANNING FOR _____ **Managing Your Time Seminar—Preparation**

TASK	SCHEDULE (Months, Weeks, Days)						TOTAL COST (FIXED)	
	JAN	FEB	MAR	APR	MAY	JUNE	MIN	MAX
SPEAKERS	SPEAKERS CONTACTED / POSSIBLE SPEAKERS	SPEAKERS COMMITTED					$750	$1,000
PROGRAM DESIGN	OUTLINE START TEXTS / NOTES	BINDERS	ORDER PRINT / BINDERS RCVD / PROGRAM DESIGNED	TEXTS AVAILABLE			800	950
PUBLICITY				PRESS RELEASES PREPARED / 1ST RELEASE	LAST RELEASE		150	200
PROMOTIONAL MATERIAL		ADVERTISING PLAN	BROCHURE / LIST ASSEMBLED 1ST MAIL	2ND MAILING	3RD MAIL		650	800
REGISTRATION			1ST REGISTRATIONS	1ST REF. MAT'L. MAILED	CLOSE REGISTRATIONS	ROSTER OF ATTENDEES	300	400
FACILITY	SELECT SITE	FLOOR PLAN / CONTRACT			SELECT MEALS	SEATING / FINAL CHECK	200	250
EQUIPMENT				LIST EQUIPMENT / LOCATE	ORDER	DELIVER / TEST	100	200
BUDGET	TENTATIVE	BREAK-EVEN SET		FINAL FIXED COST		LAST COLLECTION		

HOURS								
DOLLARS							2,950	

Probable Cost FIXED — 3,400

DESCRIPTION All Preparation needed to put on a two-day M.Y.T. Seminar on June 15-16 in Los Angeles

Figure 3

7.

It's Budget Time Again

There are probably few executives or leaders in Christian organizations who look forward to preparing the annual budget. Whether it be a local church or a large Christian service agency, there's just not much joy in going through the exercise of deciding how much money may be available to spend and how much money we can afford to spend in the next twelve months.

But it has been our experience that many Christian organizations, and particularly local churches, fail to take advantage of what can be a very revealing and stimulating exercise. Many see the budget only as a way of making some educated guesses at what fund raising targets to set and how to portion out the money.

What Are the Advantages of a Budget?

But there is potentially much more to it than that. What are the advantages of having a budget? What is it really for? First, the budget should be a *reflection* of our goals, not the basis of them. Too often churches and other Christian organizations actually do their planning by "extrapolation of last year's budget." They make a list of all the expense categories that they use: salaries, supplies, building maintenance, etc., and then discuss each expense type to decide how much they can increase it or reduce it next year. When they have added it all up, they then come to some agreement on their ability (and faith) to raise that amount. Only after that do they consider what they will actually *do* next year. Of course, it isn't usually that straightforward. Next year's needs are discussed, but they are not discussed in terms of *goals,* or even projects.

What Is the Purpose of a Budget?

What *is* the budget for? First, a reflection of our goals; but second, a forecast of need; third, one measurement of progress toward goals; fourth, an indicator of success. These four purposes indicate that the budget can be a highly understandable and communicable device for letting everyone know what's going on and what is planned for the future.

If the budget is first a reflection of goals, this assumes that we have a planning cycle within our organizations that starts with goals, moves through plans, and ends with people assignment (goal ownership) and a cost to achieve the goals. If you have been doing planning by "extrapolation of the budget," how can you change your pattern? How can you make the budgeting process both profitable and exciting?

How Can the Budget Exercise Be Profitable?

The ideal way to begin would be to try to analyze as best you can how the budget was spent both functionally and project- or goal-wise during the previous two years. For many organizations, breaking out the budget by function, i.e., departments, is not difficult. In fact, they may be doing this already.

Start by listing the budgets for the past two years

by expense type in vertical columns. (See Figure 4 on page 64) Now lay out some column headings by function. In a local church they may be "Christian education," "worship," "counseling," etc. Head the last column "miscellaneous" or "overhead." This is the place to put in everything you can't easily account for in the first columns. If you don't have any records, you may make some educated guesses. For example, in a local church there may be a paid staff of five: a pastor, associate pastor, a secretary, a clerk-typist, and a custodian. When you examine the total salary column, you will have to decide how much of their time is spent in each function. (You'd probably put the custodian's salary under "miscellaneous" because he contributed to everything that went on around the church.)

What to Do With "Miscellaneous"

It is beyond the scope of this chapter to discuss "burden" and "overhead." Suffice it to say that if the miscellaneous column is comparatively large it can be "spread" back over the other functions or projects by whatever arbitrary means seems acceptable. In our example in Figure 4, we have added it back on a percentage basis to everything except "missions." (We assumed that the amount of money going to missions was not proportionate to the "cost" of giving it."

Now at least you have made a beginning. You can talk about next year's budget by department or function.

Better to Budget by Project or Goal

But there is a better way. If you start with the projects that you want to accomplish or the goals that you want to reach, you can really do some budgeting that is directly related to where you want to go. This may seem arduous at first. But if you give the expense type sheet to each person or group that is planning a project and ask them to fill it in for their projects, when you add up all the projects, you should approximate what everyone wants to spend. *Now* if you have to trim the budget (or increase it) you can see what you are *not* going to do.

Look at this example. Suppose that you have been budgeting by total organization or function. Imagine that you have come up with a budget for the coming year that is 10 percent in excess of your anticipated income. The temptation is to first cut back every item by 10 percent. But you immediately see that unless you give the staff a salary cut, this won't work, so you try to take it out of the rest of the budget. The result may be that you end up having a staff that has no money to work with, and the project is greatly hindered.

A second example would be the same philosophy applied to a function or department. "Every department has to cut back 10 percent," might be your approach. But some functions cut back 10 percent just won't function, and you are wasting more money by just keeping them alive.

But if you have gone to the extra trouble of breaking the budget down by project or goal, these are usually a small enough percent of the total that it is practical to eliminate one that represents 10 percent and keep all the others healthy. This may be a traumatic experience, but it is a very healthy one.

A Word of Caution

In small Christian organizations where one executive, such as the pastor, covers a number of different activities or goals, it is better to keep his salary and personal expense in the "miscellaneous" category. Then when you cut out a project, you can redistribute (spread) his expense back over the remaining projects and thus avoid trying to chop out a piece of a person.

Start Early

Budgeting of this type takes time. Don't hurry it. Start your budgeting for the next year six months in advance of approval date. Begin with your goals. Circulate these and bring out conflicting interests or opinions early. After these have been resolved cost each project, including the miscellaneous. If reductions are in order, have the executive board of the organization make recommendations back to the various groups.

This Is a Process

Always see this as a process. Each year's budget should be prepared not only in light of at least two years' experience but with an additional two years' anticipation (figure 5). In other words, lay out your budget for this year with the last two years on the left and your best estimate of the following two years on the right. This will make sure that people think about the consequences of this year's budget decisions. It is also an excellent way to free people from "extrapolation of the budget" thinking as a way of planning.

ORGANIZATIONAL EXPENSE BREAKDOWN (For example only—figures are incomplete)

Expense Type	Last Year Total	Functions or Projects					Functional Totals	Miscellaneous	Next Year Total
		Worship	Education	Caring	Evangelism	Missions			
Salaries	$21,000		$8,000				$8,000	$14,000	$22,100
Insurance	275		100				100	200	300
Office Supplies	200							300	300
Material	3,200	520	2,000	240	800	300	3,860	100	3,960
Travel	900		400	500		300	1,200		1,200
Postage	600		120	240	240		600	100	700
Benevolence	22,000			1,000		23,000	24,000	200	24,200
Sub-Totals	$58,200	$4,200	$6,720	$7,045	$3,760	$27,000	$16,220	$48,725	$64,945
% of Sub-Total		20%	31%	32%	17%	N.A.		100%	
Distribution of Miscellaneous		3,244	5,028	5,190	22,557				
Totals	$58,200	$7,444	$11,748	$12,235	$6,517	$27,000			$64,945

Figure 4

64

INDIVIDUAL FUNCTION OR PROJECT COST FORECAST FOR _____

(For example only—figures are incomplete)

Expense Type	Last Year	This Year	Next Year (Budget)	% over This Year	Following Year (Plus one)	%over Last Year	Following Year (Plus two)	% over Last Year
Salaries	$20,000	$21,100	$22,100	4.7%	$31,000	40.2%	$33,000	6.4%
Insurance	255	275	300	9.0%	550	83.3%	575	4.5%
Office Supplies	200	200	300	33.3%	400	33%	450	125%
Benevolence	20,000	22,000	24,200	9.0%	27,000	11.5%	30,000	11.1%
TOTALS	$54,455	$58,200	$64,945	11.5%	$80,010	23.1%	$86,000	7.5%

Figure 5

65

8.

Let's Be Accountable

Nothing happens if someone doesn't consider himself accountable.

And yet Christian organizations in general, and local churches in particular, oftentimes are at their weakest when it comes to holding themselves accountable. One noted secular psychologist sums it up by observing that the early church discovered the tremendous social value of confessing sins to one another—being accountable. But the Roman Catholic Church came along and said that we only had to confess our sins to the priest. When the Protestants came on the scene, they made it worse! They said we only had to confess our sins to God. Then Freud came along and blew the whole thing: he said we didn't have any sins to confess!

In his book *Why Conservative Churches Are Growing* (Harper & Row Publishers), Dean Kelley observes that churches which hold their members to the highest levels of accountability are those which seem to be growing most rapidly. All of us have observed that when there is a high commitment level within any group, either to the group or to the task that the group is performing, the group appears to be more effective. Why is it then that we have such a hard time asking for and receiving accountability within Christian organizations?

Why Aren't We More Accountable?

①Probably the biggest problem is _fear_. There is a great deal of pleasure in being held accountable. It is good to share our victories with others. Yet at the same time most of us know that the joy of anticipated success can turn to ashes in the day of failure. Herein lies the tension: "success" is only possible if the possibility of failure also exists. We like to be held accountable, because we like to be recognized for what we do. And yet we are afraid to be held accountable for the same reason.

The second reason for a failure to hold people accountable is that oftentimes we just don't know _how_ to do it. We make the assumption that because we are working in a volunteer organization, such as the local church, or because we are doing "the Lord's work," that there is no way of actually demanding accountability. ③

A third reason we have run into is that some people just do not believe that holding people accountable is "Christian." "People don't do what we expect. They do what we inspect," sounds very totalitarian to them. Following up on other people is not only manipulative, but down right _non_-Christian.

Three Kinds of Accountability

There are three kinds of accountability. The first is built into the situation into which we are born. If we expect to be a part of our society, we accept the accountability that that society places upon us. We are expected to do certain things correctly and according to schedule. Taxes will come due every April. Stop lights will turn red. Such laws are powerful incentives to good "performance" on our part. And for the "twice-born" person this is also a given. "The eye cannot say to the hand, 'I have no need of you,' nor again the head to the feet, 'I have no need of you' " (1 Cor. 12:21). Accountability is assumed. It is a given, not an option.

The second kind of accountability is that which we accept when we join an organization, whether as part of our vocation or something like our local church. When we accept a job, we automatically accept responsibility to our superiors, peers, and subordinates. We may play different roles at different times, one time as leader, another time as follower. But accountability is always part of the job. Too often in Christian work we forget that.

The third kind of accountability is that which we voluntarily make to others. In many ways it is the most effective. We all seem to perform better against the goals we have set for ourselves. This third kind of accountability can operate in a number of ways. At the organizational level it works when the superior not only invites his subordinates to share in the setting of their own goals (deciding with them what he will hold them accountable for), but when the superior in turn sticks his neck out and invites his subordinates to hold *him* accountable for his goals.

How to Establish Accountability

How do we go about establishing accountability? Most developing management theory centers around the idea of mutual sharing in the setting of objectives and a continuing dialogue between the "management" and those responsible for task accomplishment. "Management by Objective" (MBO) assumes such a mutual accountability. "Objective" is a key word here. Many times we don't accept accountability because no one has defined for us what it is that we are trying to accomplish and our role in the overall task! Establishing any accountability therefore begins with goals and objectives. Every goal always has a set of subgoals or steps which must be accomplished in order to reach it. It is therefore important that each goal *and* sub-goal be assigned to an individual. There must be goal ownership. The goal only becomes operational (useful) when both the financial and human resources are available. This simple point cannot be overemphasized. If your church or Christian organization does not have clear, concise, measurable goals, you will have a great deal of difficulty placing or accepting accountability. *Accountability assumes an ability to measure.* If there are no goals, there is nothing against which to measure progress.

This brings us to a second rule for establishing good accountability. "Good goals are my goals, and bad goals are your goals," is a fact of life. We feel most responsible for those things that we have had a part in generating. If there ever was a day in volunteer organizations when most members of the organization, or local church, would automatically follow the plans laid down by others, it has long since past. People are much more likely to accept accountability if they have a part in establishing that for which they are to be held accountable.

The earlier we can bring people into the planning process, the more effective we will be. The function of leadership is to lead. Leadership needs to lay out broad purposes and directions. But effective leadership will bring in as many people as possible to refine purposes into goals and work out ways not only to meet those goals, but to measure progress (be held accountable) along the way.

Accountability Groups

Accountability groups organized around common interests or problems are used more and more. Have you heard of the Presidents' Clubs that are being formed around the United States? Each member pays a high fee (as much as $1000) to join the "club." Each man must be the president of an organization. The rules of the club specify that at each meeting one or more people will present a problem. The others will then work out a solution with him. The individual then makes a commitment to the group to go back and test their solution and report at the next meeting as to how effective it was. Professional and nonprofessional accountability groups of this type can really help us keep our goals straight. (Even without a $1000 membership fee!) Weight Watchers and Alcoholics Anonymous work on a similar principle.

This principle can be applied within an organization, as well as between organizations. A problem-solving group or meeting should never break up without ascertaining that each person in the group knows that for which he is going to be held accountable. Here the group works to hold each of its members to be accountable for the total task. This works especially well in a volunteer organization. At the end of the meeting the leader might say, "Let's see now. George, you are going to tell us at the next meeting how much it will cost to pave the lot. Jim, you are going to report back on any zoning problems. And Bob, you'll check with the other three departments involved to see if they have any objections." Now when these assignments are placed in the minutes with names of individuals, when the group meets next, the force of peer opinion will be a strong motivation to performance.

At the one-to-one, person-to-person level we should seek to be accountable to someone for as many areas of our lives as possible, and to permit others to ask us to hold them accountable. We have one mutual friend who often asks the simple question, "What can I pray about for you this week?'' We soon learned that he intended to accept responsibility to not only pray about our needs, but to ask a week later, "How did it go?" We quickly discovered not to be too glib with our prayer requests.

We Need Follow-up

Good!

Placing or accepting accountability is not enough. Someone needs to be responsible (accountable) to take necessary follow-up and see how things are going. There are some good reasons:

- We need to make sure the agreed upon goals still exist.

- We need to find out whether the instructions given were adequate and clear. Perhaps the person only assumed that he understood what was the task, and he is proceeding in quite the wrong direction.

- It may be that the person has encountered problems which he either does not recognize or about which he is reticent to ask for help.

- It may be that someone else is dependent upon this particular task, and they need to be assured that the task has actually been accomplished so that they can begin theirs.

- It strengthens the relationship between individuals by demonstrating that one person thinks it's important enough to inquire as to what happened.

- It builds in a feeling of responsibility, one toward the other.

- It shows that the task is important. We are bombarded by so many demands on our time that we have a subconscious way of measuring the importance of the task by how much interest is shown in it by others.

How to Follow-up

There are many ways to follow up. The best way is to set follow-up dates along the way. Build in these check points during the initial planning, and agree upon them with people with whom you are working. Display them in a way that everybody can see progress. Build in a reporting system so that people can *follow up on themselves*. Know the people you work with well enough to understand what motivates them. Some will require a lot of follow-up, others very little.

Follow up in time to recover if something has gone amiss. There's little point in calling the day before something needs to be done if it takes three days to do it.

Being Accountable Pays Off

Holding others accountable and being held accountable is at the root of the life that is Christian. Our Lord is going to hold us accountable for all the gifts he has given us. "By this all men will know that you are my disciples, if you have love for one another" (John 13:35). That kind of love demands accountability. But the rewards are great, not only in satisfaction of accomplishment, but in our relationship with one another.

9.

Is It Time for an Audit?

Most of us are familiar with the idea of a financial audit. Periodically, usually every year, an accredited outside organization is asked to come in and review our personal or organizational accounts. The purpose of the audit is to make sure that our financial operations are being carried out in a technical and businesslike manner and that the finances of the company are in good order. Are we making a profit, or are we experiencing a loss? When we compare our financial performance to last year, are we improving or falling behind?

It goes without saying that every Christian organization should have a responsible auditor review its finances each year. His findings should be made public for all those who have a need to know.

Organizational Audit

Perhaps not so familiar to many people is the organization or management audit. The basic idea is the same. Each area of the organization's operations is reviewed in terms of the stated intentions of the program. Are we making a "profit," or are we experiencing a "loss"? Are we improving over last year, or falling behind?

To many people, this is a startling, if not a frightening idea. The idea of someone else prying into the everyday operations of the organization or into personal successes or failures does not sound too attractive. But we should not be afraid of a management audit. Quite the contrary. We should encourage every opportunity to do a review of where we've been, where we are, and where we are going.

The Management Audit

Just as any good financial audit must be based upon predetermined budgets, so a management audit must start much earlier with established management goals and objectives. The goals and objectives of top management are the goals and objectives of the organization. These are the *primary* goals into which those and all of the sub-units of the organization should fit their goals. So the first question is, "How are we doing, or how did we do, in the reporting period against our overall goals?" Is the trend to exceed our goals year by year, or are we falling behind? Do we have an adequate number of milestones against which to measure progress, and are we doing so? With this understanding of the situation we can move on to ask some other questions that impact on overall management.

Do we believe that we have adequate staff to carry out our overall objectives? Do we have too much staff? Are there some staff members who don't fit? Does each staff member have a job description, and has this been reviewed during the past year? (See below under personal audit.)

What about our reporting system? Do the *top* executives and the other managers of the organization really know what is happening? Do other people in the organization know what management is thinking? One good way of auditing this is to ask each manager or administrator to describe the responsibilities of his subordinates. Then in turn ask the subordinates to describe their own responsibilities. If good communication exists, most of the time the description of what the manager thinks the subordinate is supposed to be doing, and what the subordinate thinks he is supposed to be doing, will be pretty close. (Note that this concept can be worked down through all levels of the organization.) What kind and how many reports have been issued, both down the line and up the line, during the course of the year? Do these reports reflect and discuss the goals of the organization and its program, or are they generalized discussions about past activities?

What is being done and how effective is the program of staff training? Is there an individual responsible to see that staff training needs are identified to management, and each individual has an opportunity for learning? What do the individuals of the management staff say about what they have learned during the past period, and why they think they have learned it? Do they feel like they are progressing in their abilities, or stagnating? (This will again raise the question of whether each staff person is in the right spot, needs to be moved, replaced, or supported with additional staff.)

Are facilities and equipment adequate to fulfill present and future needs? In the long run, good equipment is cheaper than inexpensive equipment. Are any frustrations being experienced by the organization or the individuals on the staff because of lack of equipment? Do we have too much equipment? Are there excess facilities which are really a burden, or are no longer needed? Are we operating equipment or facilities which could be better subcontracted outside or vice versa? What is it about the present environment that makes it conducive to more effective work? What could be done to improve the environment?

Program Audit

Programs are the tasks that the organization is carrying out to meet its goals and objectives. Too often, however, it is possible for a program to be operating without a stated goal. Therefore, the first question of a program audit is "Are the goals clearly stated, and are they obviously related to the goals and objectives of the organization?" If they are not, why are they not? Have they always been this way, or has there been a drift away from goals? Are the goals so general as to not be meaningful, or were they communicated?

Is the program justifying its existence? Should it be continued during the following year? Could it be done in a better way? Each year there should be a given number of programs that are eliminated. Which ones are candidates this year? (In order to be able to do "more," often we have to eliminate to make room for new things.)

Personal Audit

It is all too easy for a pastor or a Christian leader to be threatened by the idea of an outsider making a personal audit of his performance. But don't be threatened. The result will be your own strengthening. More than anyone else, the Christian manager or pastor must be willing to set personal goals and evaluate his own performance, and have it evaluated by others. The setting of personal goals is probably more difficult than the setting of organizational goals.

The personal evaluation or audit should begin with a job description. What is it that the leader or program manager is supposed to do? The writing of a job, or position, description is covered in chapter 20.

Suffice it to say here that it will vary between individuals and tasks. But regardless of what form or format is used for the writing of the job description, it should be a reasonably clear statement of what the results of the individual's involvement in the organization will be. We need to go beyond the *function* of the individual to the *purpose* of the task. This is why they are job descriptions, rather than a description of the individual. To put it another way, we should describe the position that we want filled, and then attempt to audit the individual against this description. This, of course, assumes that there has been prior agreement on the part of the individual, that this is indeed the particular position description against which he is going to operate.

It should be remembered that the purpose of the audit is not to keep the individual honest, but to give an accurate picture of where he is heading, and where he may need help. This assumes a mutual trust between the one being audited and the auditor.

Financial Audit

It goes without saying that a financial audit should be made at least every year for every church and Christian organization. However, too often this is done in a haphazard manner or by volunteers. This is no place, however, for amateurs. Do it right. Have it done by someone who knows how. Remember you're responsible to the Lord for the use of his riches. There's no other area in society in which people are more sensitive.

Who Should Do the Auditing?

There are professional firms who will do a management

audit that covers all aspects of the organization—management, program, personnel, and finance. Such organizations are expensive, and we personally know of none that specialize in the auditing of Christian organizations. For the financial audit, a professional firm should certainly be used. You will discover that the more well-known and experienced firms are not necessarily more expensive than the smaller ones. Encourage and anticipate that the auditor will find areas for improvement, and suggest that he give you recommendations as to how next year's audit can be made to move more easily, be made more clear to those who will read it, and will assist the organization in operating more smoothly.

There are firms that specialize in assisting in the writing of position descriptions, and in doing personnel and organizational evaluations. These can be very helpful at times, particularly if the organization is in a transition or a growth period.

Some firms specialize in doing audits of computer systems, work-flow systems, and internal communication. Many such firms will also offer training in how to improve operations in a particular area that they have audited. It should be recognized here that when a firm does both auditing and training there is a potential conflict of interest. At the same time it should be recognized that the firm that has done the auditing is in a much better position to suggest improvements than one which must work with someone else's audit. In the area of program and personnel audit, the whole concept of management by objective (MBO) is designed to give such a built-in evaluating system. Each leader or manager should have a time, at least each year, when he reviews the position description of his subordinates with them and evaluates their performance against their job description. The MBO concept assumes that the initial task description will include within it milestones for periodic review.

But who audits the pastor or the top executive of the organization? This is a sensitive area that needs careful handling. The wise leader will insist that an individual or small committee from his church or organizational board, or from within the congregation, be set up to meet with him periodically to review his progress. One pastor we know facilitates this process for his congregation by submitting his resignation each year. It is obvious that such an auditor or group of auditors must not be yes-men, nor should they, at the same time, be antagonistic. Rather, they should be looked upon as people who will have a sensible view of the leader's job, and will look upon it as their task to assist him in doing it better.

In Conclusion

The audit of where we've been, where we are, and where we're going is a sign of a healthy organization and a healthy individual. An open discussion of the need and how-to of a regular organization and personnel audit is very helpful in clearing the air within an organization and opening up new lines of communication.

A leadership which demonstrates its willingness to stick its neck out in faith—as to what it believes God wants the organization to do—and is willing to have others evaluate its performance against its stated goals, is the kind of leadership that most of us want to follow.

10.

Management By Objectives

What difficulty we have in describing most organizations, particularly Christian ones! When asked to describe their organization, many people respond by talking about the internal relationships, who reports to whom, who is responsible for what. Others talk about what the organization believes, what it stands for. Still others will describe the organization in terms of what it is doing. They may break it down to its many functional relationships.

If asked to draw a *picture* of an organization, almost anyone with a business background will automatically revert to the relational model, in other words, the organization chart. Usually this is viewed as a pyramid with a "leader" or board or committee at the top of the pile. The diagram might look something like this:

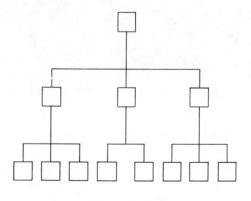

Since most organizations are created to accomplish a task, or for the upbuilding of their members, it is surprising that people continue to use an organization chart when asked to picture their organization. If instead of describing the organization in terms of the relationship of the various positions in the organization, we describe it in the terms of its purposes and goals, might not it look something like this?

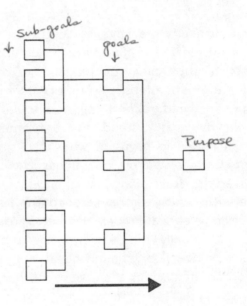

Here we have the major purpose or purposes of the organization "leading" the goals and the sub-goals of the organization. It is somewhat like a dynamic model in which the purposes are pulling the goals and sub-goals along. Such a model is far more useful than the organization chart for it depicts what *should be* happening within the organization rather than the status quo.

Management by Objectives

This leads us into our subject: Management by Objectives (MBO). Hopefully, leaders of the Christian community are getting over some of their reticence about using the word "management." However, for many it still has vestiges of manipulation and control which they believe have no part in a Christian organization. But Christian organizations should have no trouble with *objectives!* Through the ages the church has seen itself involved with a *mission*. And what is more clear-cut, more definite, more purposeful than mission?

There are many ways of thinking about the management of an organization. Christian organizations have a particularly difficult task because they do not have the clear-cut "bottom line" evaluation of the profit-making organization. A profit-making organization ultimately rises or falls on one simple question: Did it make a profit? The Christian organization has no such clear-cut definition of performance. Therefore, it tends to functionalism and institutionalism, becoming ingrown upon itself, and operating for its own good rather than the original purposes of its founders. (See chapter 11 on Self-Renewal.) Therefore, management by objective is even more appropriate for the Christian organization than it is for the profit-making organization.

What Is Management by Objective?

Basically it is a philosophy of management which says one begins to think about the organization in terms of its overall purposes, that these purposes are then reduced to accomplishable and measurable goals, and that finally the

1) Purpose
2) acc. & measurable goals
3) objectives to accomplish goals

85

key individuals within the organization write objectives as
to how they are going to accomplish these goals. The idea
is not new. It was first popularized by Peter Drucker in his
Practice of Management (Harper and Row) when he described "Management by Objective and Self-Control." In
principle it is very simple. In practice it is very difficult to
carry out, particularly in the not-for-profit organization.

Assumptions

Management by objective makes a number of assumptions about the organization. First, it assumes that the
organization has clearly defined purposes and goals. Second, it assumes that there is an internal agreement as to
the fact that these purposes and goals are the way the
organization should move. Third, it assumes a commitment
to performance against goals and purposes from the top
of the organization down. Fourth, it assumes that a motivation of performance against goals is a basic criteria of
evaluation of individuals and units within the organization.
If one or more of these assumptions is not true, then there
are a number of things which must go before the installation of an MBO system within an organization. These will
be discussed below.

How to Begin

Let's assume that as you look at the organization of your
church or Christian organization you conclude that it could
become more effective using this approach in accomplishing its task. What should you do? Where should you
begin? First, there should be an increasingly broadening
discussion about the concept throughout the organization.
If the idea is initiated outside the top leadership, then
there needs to be a careful (and patient) introduction of
the idea. This means doing some homework (see suggested

reading below) and perhaps some outside counsel. When one starts asking questions about the worth or effectiveness of any group, there is bound to be concern and perhaps fear. After all, none of us likes the thought that we might be measured and found wanting. Before I am willing to submit to this type of scrutiny I have to believe that it will not only improve the effectiveness of the group but my own effectiveness as well.

Work on the Purposes and Goals

Sometimes it is startling to discover that we really don't have agreement on where we are going and how we are going to get there. Take your time. Gather statements from as many significant persons as you can. Don't overlook the existing organizational structure. Ask each subgroup to state its own purposes and objectives and to what higher objectives these relate. (For this discussion we are using "objective" and "goal" interchangeably as a *measurable event* and reserving the word "purpose" for the higher aim or direction that may be clear as to its worth, but not necessarily measurable as such. "To give glory to God" is a purpose. "To have a new office in Kattar with three people by January 1" is an objective.)

Obtain General Agreement on Objectives

What is needed is a clear set of objectives on a yearly basis for the next five years. It is recognized that these will have to be reviewed and modified regularly. It is recognized that they may change drastically. The point is that we all know where we are going as of now so we can discuss where and why we are departing from them. The assumption is that this will uncover missing areas of effort or weaknesses that can be bolstered.

Again, take your time. Unless the organization is facing

an immediate crisis, work to get as much understanding and agreement as possible. Listen to differing viewpoints.

Relate Individual Objectives into a Whole

The organization chart on page 21 illustrates what we mean. The major objectives should fit together. If there are objectives that just don't seem to fit anywhere, perhaps you have discovered some work that just doesn't need to be done.

Reach Agreement on Accountability

This is the hardest part and the heart of the MBO concept. Unless we are willing to be *individually* accountable, we can have little organizational accountability. We each need to see where we fit and what we do has an impact on the whole.

A great deal has been said about written performance objectives and job descriptions. Read the literature. The basic idea is to review with each leadership person the task to (1) reach agreement that this *is* their task, (2) mutually develop milestones or steps that will be a measure of how and if the task is being carried out, and (3) set up a review system to measure performance.

Measure Progress

What seems so simple in theory now meets the hard pavement of practicality. There needs to be a series of review times or meetings during which the team or the individual is going to state its performance. These need to be scheduled close enough that it is still possible to take some corrective action, but not so close as to remove responsibility. The times may vary with person and project. For example, in a local church the installation of a new curriculum in eight months may require a monthly review, while planning a special Christmas service should be looked at each week. In a mission agency a training program for new recruits might need weekly review. A program to establish a new work in a different country in three years might need only a bi-monthly review.

Discuss Individual Performance

It is difficult for us all to talk about how another person is doing his job. The major advantage of MBO is that it seeks to have the individual participate not only in the planning of his program, but how he (and others) will know how he is doing. By holding a joint review against a written statement of personal objective, the focus is directed away from the individual to the task. This still doesn't make it easy, of course, but it does help the individual to point out his own areas of weakness and make suggestions for strengthening them.

The Advantages of Management by Objective

When an organization calls itself and its members to account for what it is doing, it places a high priority on accomplishing that for which the organization was called into being.

A continuous review of performance against objectives points out sub-organizations and departments that need to be modified or eliminated and others which need to be called into being. The organization can thus be viewed as a body which is continually being renewed by the death of some cells and their replacement with others.

Individual commitment is strengthened and individuals whose task is accomplished or who are working on the wrong task can be identified and helped.

Management by Objective

George Odiorne's *Management By Objectives* (Pitman Publishing Corporation) was the first book dedicated entirely to this concept.

W. J. Reddin's *Effective Management by Objectives: The 3D Method of MBO* (McGraw-Hill Book Company) is an excellent book on how to install MBO in an organization and some of the difficulties of doing so.

11.

Self-Renewal

The world is full of dying organizations. Once they were young and vibrant and growing. But now they are dying. To the casual observer they may appear to be doing important things and carrying on "business as usual." And yet they are dying. The enthusiasm that marked their early days of growth is gone. The challenge to *be* and to *do* has been replaced by the day-to-day monotony of "doing the work."

There are churches that are dying.

There are missions that are dying.

There are all sorts of Christian organizations that are dying. Many of them should.

Many have accomplished the task they set out to do and should now be accorded a triumphal memorial service. There was a time and there was a place for them. But that time has passed. They have become absorbed with their *function* rather than their goals, and it is time to call it quits.

The problem with these organizations is they have forgotten that *the purpose of organizing is to accomplish something.* Now they have either done what they set out to do, or it has become obvious that they never will.

But what of the organization whose goal still lies up ahead? What of the organization that has grown and moved ahead but now seems to be bogged down in the ritualistic business of "We have always done it this way"? Can such organizations be renewed? If so, how? What are the elements of a self-renewing organization?

Phases of Growth

Every organization is different, but there are some generalizations that help us understand why some move ahead while others falter. Organizations seem to go through similar phases. When "growth" is charted, many show typical patterns of growth, plateau, and so on. The plateaus appear to be necessary times of consolidation. After a surge of expansion, energies need to be turned toward how to work what is essentially a new organization.

Many times these phases require a different style of leadership. Quite often the Christian organization is founded by an individual with above average vision and single-mindedness. In the early life of the organization the founder has his hand in everything and quite naturally makes most of the decisions. But if "success" in the organization is accompanied by financial and/or personnel growth, the day comes when decision making must be delegated.

This delegation may be explicit or implied, but it must happen. The leader may not even be aware of it. Human organizations are amazingly adaptive. But happen it must.

This is the end of the early growth phase. Now more and more of the organizational functions tend to be divided by type. Groups of specialists emerge, specialists in things like education, evangelism, administration. During this phase it is easy for the organization to turn inward and to become absorbed with its technique rather than its goals. Standing committees are formed. Departments are added. What started out as a part-time volunteer running a mimeograph machine turns into a printing department.

This is really a new and different kind of organization, and it requires a different style of leadership. Management skills are needed to supplement leadership gifts. Some leaders grow with the organization they have founded. They are probably a minority. Others become frustrated or overwhelmed with all the details of keeping things going.

For a while the organization will run and organize itself. But as this happens the Kingdom Complex sets in. Individuals become concerned with their own task. Since the original goals of the organization are not being continuously held aloft by the leadership, people set their own goals, and these typically have to do with *function* rather than accomplishment.

The Danger of Doing Good Things

The phases we have described above are part of a repetitive process. They tend to repeat themselves as the organization grows. Unless some form of renewal takes place, almost every organization will become loaded down with good people doing good things that have nothing to do with the goals at which the organization is purportedly aiming. The for-profit organization has a built-in corrective. It must supply a desirable product or service, or it will be forced out of business. Unfortunately, not-for-profit organizations, such as government bureaus and Christian groups, can continue to survive because their resources are dependent not on their ability to do their task, but rather on their ability to convince their supporters of the worthiness of their cause.

Thus we find some foreign missions operating good-sized overseas staffs the same way they did fifteen, twenty, or even thirty years ago. And we find local churches with excellent reputations who are content to nurture their members while the number of new Christians coming into their midst is small if any.

What Is the Remedy?

This is an all-too-brief description of the disease and some of its causes. What of the remedy?

Clear goals, ladies and gentlemen! Clear goals! Goals that are reviewed regularly to see if they are still viable and discarded if they are not. This must be the foundation. The pioneer leader knew what he wanted to do and where he wanted to go. He may not have done the best job of enunciating the details, but by the very force of his person he carried others along. But when the pioneer days are passed, the organization must provide what the individual no longer can, a sense of purpose and direction that can be felt through all its ranks.

It cannot be said too often: *goal setting is a process.* There will always be more to do than we can possibly accomplish. What are the highest priority goals, the ones for *this* day and *this* need? And consequently, which ones are now no longer appropriate and should thus be abandoned (even though they have never been met)? It is always too soon to quit, but it's seldom too late to change direction.

Some Christian organizations, especially local churches, find themselves in a box built by the founders within which it is difficult to move. A constitution that seemed ageless in the 30s may hamstring the church of the 70s. This is a good warning for the future. If you are part of forming a new organization, and if a constitution is needed, perhaps the first article should be, "This constitution shall become null and void five years after its adoption." It is always easy to readopt the old one if it is still current.

Keep Goals Dynamic

So begin by keeping the organization's goals dynamic and open to change. And next work on "posteriorities," those things you are *not* going to do next year. Few organizations can continue to add new projects without stopping some old ones. If each project is given a termination date, the problem can be avoided, but if there are a large number of open-ended projects, set up a review time at least each year to discuss posteriorities.

Reexamine Functions

This is a good time to look at the organization functionally. Are there certain functions that could either be eliminated or better done outside the organization? Each functional department or group should be examined in terms of the *goals of the organization*. How did it happen to be established in the first place? Are the reasons still valid? What is its true cost? In an organization that may be using volunteers, this is difficult to figure. Consider not only cost but organizational effectiveness. For example, it may be much less expensive to do in-house printing using volunteers, but the quality may be such as to communicate the wrong message. Where the organization does not use volunteers, don't forget to add the "overhead"— the floor space, lights, taxes, etc., that having such a function requires.

Emphasize Form Not Structure

If we begin with goals and then tailor our functions to meet those goals, it follows that the organization structure will need to be modified continually to enable those functions to take place. *Enable* is a good word. Organizations should be enabling environments, places where people can do the best job possible. A great deal of work has been done and is being done on the nature of "effective" versus "ineffective" organizations. About the only rule-of-thumb that has emerged is that their shape needs to fit the nature of the task and the style of the people working in them. Self-renewing organizations, almost by definition, are continually modifying their structure to those needs.

What Do Others Think?

What do others think about your organization and what it is doing? What's your reputation in the marketplace? Find opportunities to meet with others in the same business, whether that business be ministering to children, running an educational institution or foreign missions. How do you compare? What's their experience? How do they think about you?

Encourage Self-Renewal at All Levels

How? By encouraging people to reexamine their own goals and the goals of their unit or department. *Set aside time* for the evaluation process. If the leadership doesn't give it priority, no one else will either. Look for innovation and innovators. There is nothing more frustrating than someone with twenty more ideas than you can implement. But find ways to "store" them. After all, if it's a good idea that fits your organizational goals, it's more of a question of "when, and how much" than "if."

Self-Renewal Is a State of Mind

In the final analysis self-renewal depends on an attitude, and that primarily of its top management. Openness to the future, openness to what God intends them to be, a confidence that Spirit-empowered people whom the Bible describes as a "body" can continue to grow—these are the characteristics of the Christian leaders of self-renewal.

Additional Reading

By all means read John Gardner's classic work *Self Renewal* (Harper and Row Publishers).

Many attempts are being made to consider self-renewal of organizations by those who are practicing "organizational development." Warren Bennis' *Organization Development: Its Nature, Origin and Prospects* is a small paperback published by Addison Wesley which will give you a good introduction to the whole subject.

12.

Doing or Being

There are two distinctives which should be the hallmark of any Christian organization, whether it be a local church or a worldwide enterprise. The first is quite apparent. It is the *purpose* of the organization. Indeed it is that very purpose that delineates the organization as Christian. The second may not be so apparent. It is the relationships that exist within the organization, how the people within the organization view one another and act toward one another.

The same two distinctives should be the hallmark of any Christian *leader*. The Christian leader is a man or a woman with a Christian *purpose*. A Christian leader is a man or a woman with Christian relationships.

Doing and Being

There is always a tension between what we believe we should *do* (our tasks) and what we believe God would have us to *be* (our relationship to others). This tension exists within the Christian organization, and it exists within the life of the Christian leader. We'll briefly discuss both of these situations.

The Organization

Organizations are the outward manifestation of a shared purpose. Any time two or more people agree to work together toward a common goal, an organization exists. All organizations are basically relationships. An organization chart is an attempt to describe these relationships, usually in terms of authority and/or responsibility. How these relationships are structured and how they are viewed by the people within the organization will determine the character of that organization.

When we look to the New Testament for descriptions of how Christians should relate to one another, we are startled by the tremendous contrast between what our experience tells us an organization should be like and the description of that ultimate organization, the church. Instead of finding a pyramidal structure in which those further down on the pyramid are subservient to those above, we are given the model of the human body (1 Corinthians 12). We discover that how this body functions is determined completely by how each member functions. We are told that there are no unimportant members. In fact, our worldly concepts are completely turned upside down as we are told that the "inferior" parts of the body are worthy of more honor. And it is because of this that we are to weep with those who weep and rejoice with those who rejoice (Romans 12:15).

Within this body it is assumed that there is a high level of communication, in that in some sense all members are in relationship to all other members, but especially in close relationship with some. The implication is that members within the organization are to be treated like adults, rather than children, that they are expected to assume responsibility and to carry it out.

Being, Not Doing

It is interesting to note that the New Testament has a great deal to say about how we are to relate to each other and very little to say about the ultimate purpose of this relationship in terms of *accomplishment*. A startling example is how little the New Testament says about getting on with the task of evangelism. Rather we discover that evangelism will be the natural outflowing of the relationship that exists. Jesus sums this up in his high priestly prayer when he notes that the way the world will come to believe that he is the Son of God will be because his disciples have the same relationship which he has with his Father (John 17:21).

But How?

That's all very well and good, we may reply, but how do you make it work? People are naturally sinful. If we attempt to have an organization in which everybody is running things, people are certain to take advantage of us. How far *should* our responsibility go toward caring for employees? To what extent can we treat people as adults and brothers (rather than children) and expect them to act that way too?

It has been fascinating over a period of years to watch secular management theorists come closer and closer to the New Testament model of the church as an organization. A detailed description of this development is beyond the scope of this book. (See the writings of Abraham Maslow, A. A. C. Brown, Paul Gellerman, Elton Mayo, Robert W. White, Douglas McGregor, Chris Argyris, Frederick Herzberg, Rensis Likert, and others.) However, there is a growing body of literature and experience which demonstrates that there is a direct relationship between the effectiveness—output, goal achievement, success—of organizations and the degree to which individuals within the organization are dealt with as valued, mature adults. Note that this does not mean that the organization exists for the benevolent good of the individuals within it. It does mean that in whatever degree possible within the confines of education, experience, and ability, members of the organization should perceive themselves as *participating* in the organization in a way that determines the effectiveness of that organization.

How to Begin

Too often the leaders of Christian organizations come to their positions because of qualifications other than those which would equip them to be thoughtful managers. And organizations have a history of growing in the same haphazard fashion. Unfortunately, too often when the organization views itself as "successful," it attributes this to the rather nebulous "blessing of God" and consequently fails to analyze what elements God used! The highly educated, cohesive core of men and women who have been responsible for the early effectiveness of an organization can quickly become diluted as the organization grows in scope and size. What can we do to rebuild into Christian organizations that sense of "life in the body" which existed in its early days?

Sharing and Accountability

Begin with sharing the goal-setting experience. (See chapter 1.) This is not an easy task. You may discover that people within the organization will have a tremendous "show me" attitude. Their past experience tells them that very seldom are their ideas acted upon. You may also have difficulty with *yourself.* Your sense of leadership may be threatened. You may feel that you are losing control.

Take your time. It takes years to change the character of an organization. As you work with establishing a set of integrated goals at all levels within the organization, expect that it will be one to two years before people really see how they fit in.

Expect and demand accountability, not in the sense of threat for failure to perform, but in the sense that if we really believe in what we are doing and believe we have contributed toward it, we *will* assume that we are accountable for results and will expect that others will hold us accountable. Start "acting as if." Act as if you expected contributions from other members of the organization. Act as if you valued their opinion. Act as if they were adults, not children who need to be told everything that they are to do. Act as if their well-being is as important to you as the well-being of the organization. Act as if you expect to hold them to account for the goals they have set and to hold you to account for the goals that you have set. Act as if they are important enough so that you need to share with them where the organization is in its progress towards its goals.

Task vs. People

There will be no easy answers. On the one hand, the people cannot be sacrificed for "the good of the organization." On the other hand, if the *goals and purposes* of the organization are sacrificed for the good of the individuals, then the organization will cease to function.

One of the reasons that the local church is the most complex of all human organizations is that it has set for itself two purposes which tend to oppose one another: the purpose of being a servant to the world in work and witness, and the purpose of building up the individual members of the body in terms of their well-being. This is why we believe that to the degree that we understand how to be effective leaders of a local church, we will learn to be effective as leaders in *any* organization.

The Christian Leader

The Christian *leader*, too, will find the same tension between doing and being in his or her own life. People extend to us the right to lead on the basis of their perception of not only what we have done, but how we have done it, not only what we do, but what we *are*. The Christian leader must build, develop, and carefully guard his relationships at all levels of life.

The New Testament gives as one of the qualifications of a leader that he must be able to manage his household well. As is obvious from the rest of the New Testament, this does not mean how well he can dictate and control his family, but rather how well he has developed the relationships within his family that are Christ-honoring and people-honoring. The same *principle* can obviously be applied to women (Proverbs 31:10).

We believe that the first three levels of Christian priority are first, commitment to the Person of Christ; second, commitment to the body of Christ; and third, commitment to the work of Christ. There is no doubt that the New Testament calls us to be willing to sacrifice houses, families, and lands to follow Christ. But as we have noted above, the *work* of Christ will flow forth from the relationships that exist. Too often we have heard Christian leaders say, "What I do as a leader is so important that I must sacrifice my family." If by this he or she means that the work of Christ is more important than the body of Christ, we must protest that this is not the view of the New Testament. The Bible considers our relationships as being more important than our accomplishments. God will get his work done! He does not demand of us that we accomplish great things. He demands of us that we strive for excellence in our relationships.

How This Might Work

Are you a goal-oriented person or a person-oriented (relationship) person? One way to find out is to take a look at your calendar. How much time have you been spending with your spouse, your children, your brothers and sisters in Christ? If you looked at your appointment book right now, would you find dates with your husband or wife, dates with your teenage daughter or son, times on the calendar to be with other people to help them meet their goals? Is your calendar so full that there is no "unscheduled" time when other people can get with you? Is every evening of the week scheduled with "work"? Change your priorities! Start scheduling times for relationships, both with your family, or other members of the body, and with people within your organization. God wants you to have these relationships. (It's OK—really.)

Build Relationships

You might want to consider three different kinds of relationships that are tremendously useful to any Christian leader.

First is the need for a Barnabas, a "son of consolation," someone to whom you can go, openly share where you're at and seek wise counsel and prayer support. Too often pastors particularly fail to develop such a relationship with a person within their own congregation or fellowship.

Second, build a relationship with a peer group—a small

group of men and women to hold you accountable and whom you can hold accountable as fellow members of Christ. Find times when you can get together on a regular basis to share your life.

Third, find a Timothy, someone into whom you can build your years of experience, someone that you can help mature in Christ and in his role of leadership.

In all of this, remember the different relationship roles that you play. Every leader at some time is a follower. Learning to be a good follower is a major step to being a good leader.

PART TWO

Leadership Skills

13.

Communicate, or Else...

An effective organization needs clear and communicable *goals*, adequate *resources*, *motivated people*, and *good communication*. If the objectives of the group are understood and accepted by all of its members, and if they have the corporate resources to attain their objectives, *then* what each member of the group needs is information on what to do, how to do it, when to do it, and where to do it. In order to maintain his commitment to the task, he also needs to know what progress he and the rest of the organization are making toward reaching their goals.

Good communication, not structure, is the cement that holds any organization together. Given the above mix of ingredients almost any *structure* will do the job.

But communication is a very difficult business at best, and it becomes particularly difficult in a volunteer organization, and especially that most complicated volunteer organization, the local church!

How easy it is to forget that imparting information is not communication. It's a funny thing how most of us believe that if the person we are working with only had all the same facts (information) that we have, then "he'll see it my way." But most of the time he probably won't! Each one of us looks at the world through a different set of eyes which have somehow been conditioned to see certain things and overlook others.

What happens when you try to impart information to someone? Communication begins to take place when an idea or "message" is formed in the mind of the "receiver." His human radar gathers data from all its surroundings— what's being said, the situation within which it's being said, who's saying it, his past experience, how he feels that day, his own self-image, and so on. The information you transmit is only the raw material he works with.

Let's look at the process a moment. Figure 6 is a simple diagram of some of the things that go on. (See next page.)

The "receiver" may have heard everything that was said, but communication only occurs when he assigns *meaning* to the content. On the basis of this understanding he makes a response (feedback), and the process repeats itself again.

One reason why Harris' book *I'm OK—You're OK* has been at the top of the best-seller list is because it helps us understand why some of our messages get assigned such unintended meanings. This understanding should in turn encourage us to keep checking out what the other person intends to say: "Now, what I hear you saying is . . ." By repeating back the message is another form we make sure we understand what the speaker intended, and we help him listen to what *he* said!

So much for theory. What does this have to say about Christian leadership?

In some ways the Christian leader has two strikes against him in the communication process. First, he comes from a tradition of authoritarian pronouncement where abstract ideas are held to have meaning in themselves. "Thus saith the Lord . . ." does have a way of silencing our fellow believers! Second, there is a tacit assumption in a Christian organization that we *do* understand each other because

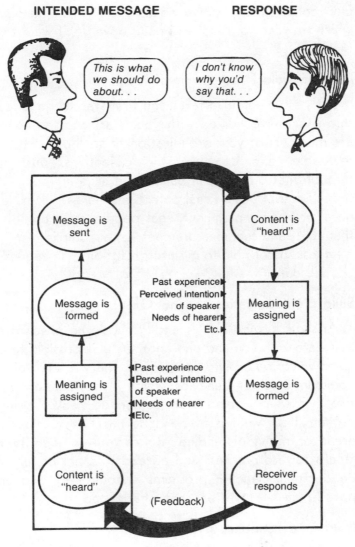

Figure 6

we share a common belief in one God and Savior. We dislike to question another Christian's motives or actions. But too often in fact we hold widely diverging opinions which we keep to ourselves because we don't want to rock the boat.

How to Unlock Communication

Let's assume you've taken the first step of good leadership—you have worked with your staff and the appropriate members of your organization to spell out some clear, realizable, and communicable objectives. Just going through that process can build some excellent communication bridges, because real objectives—ones that have real dates for accomplishment, real people assigned to carry them out, and real measurements of accomplishment—are a lot less susceptible to misinterpretation than vague "purposes." But now what?

Build Communication around Objectives

Analyze the individuals and groups who need to communicate with you and one another. Is it possible to *build communication around objectives?* This will tend to center communication on behavior, which is much easier to identify than what's going on in someone's head! Talking together about what is to be done has a way of reducing areas of misunderstanding. Be careful to identify milestones toward progress and agreed to times of reporting, on decisions needed, problems encountered, and anticipated plans—as well as what's happened.

Build in a Feedback System

Have staff and committees report regularly against objectives. Don't just report what's happened. Good reports should (1) tell the leader or committee what decisions are needed; (2) what problems are foreseen; (3) what is planned for the immediate future; and (4) what has been done. (No sense in telling everyone the barn door was left open after the horse has gone!)

Establish Regular Channels for How-Goes-It Information

There is a lot of information that is needed as background to the current major events that are occurring in the group. Gossip and rumor find a ready ear if the members of the group don't believe they are in-the-know. Weekly news bulletins, special announcements on events or progress, a monthly letter from the leader giving his assessment, all meet some of these needs. Find someone in the organization who seems to know everything that's going on and give him the task of compiling local organization news items. Make sure you give your own regular progress report.

Recognize Different Levels of Communication

And be careful not to confuse them. We have been conditioned by our society to equate the importance of a communication with the volume level and the source. Important communication must look and sound important! But be selective and don't use the same big guns all the time. *Too many* important looking messages (special letters, announcements, etc.) will soon require that the really important ones sound like the finale of Tschaikovsky's "1812 Overture." On the other side, important messages buried in the background level of weekly news will not only be overlooked, but not considered important.

Plan Your Communication

In order to accomplish the objective that lies before us, *who* needs to know? What group? department? key individuals? what part of the constituency? *What* do they need to know? This immediately raises the question of *how much*. There's no sense in giving everyone all the data if only a few need to know all the details. Take time to break it down into appropriate packages.

Next, consider how you will make the communication. Phone call? Letter? Memo? All three? Presentation? How? Last, remember the diagram in Figure 6. How will you know that communication (the transfer of meaning) has actually taken place?

Be As Redundant As Possible

Christian organizations talk a great deal about efficiency and avoiding duplication. In his book *Parish Planning*, Lyle Schaller points out that the one place we need all the duplication and redundancy we can get is in the area of communication. Individuals differ tremendously in how they "receive." Some are readers, some are listeners. Some always seem to have their antennas out searching for data. Others seem to have their internal microphone turned off most of the time.

Spend Money on Internal Communication

A volunteer organization's lifeblood is its members. These members need to be informed, instructed, motivated, and listened to. That takes time, money, and energy. Put it in the budget! It's amazing how a local church will spend thousands of dollars to support a cause at home or abroad, but can't bring itself to spend 5 percent of that on educating and informing those who must continue to support the cause. (Church missionary committees, take note!)

Educate People to Communicate Better

Some of us just need to learn how to listen better. It

takes practice! Others need to discover how people are hearing *them*. One valuable learning device is self-evaluation of meetings. Leave some time at the end of a meeting (perhaps ten minutes) to discuss how the meeting was conducted: Did it serve its purpose? Did people seem to be understanding one another? How could it be improved? You'll be surprised at how easily people will identify blocks to communication. Sometimes it's helpful to appoint one person as an interpreter, to stay outside the discussion as an observer, and then help get the ball rolling by giving an evaluation at the close of the meeting.

There is a growing body of individuals who are available to assist volunteer organizations in sharpening their internal communication skills. Consider locating some of the resource centers and discussing such training with them.

Give It Time

People who work together day after day find it easier to meet and communicate with one another than volunteers who may only see each other once a week and meet as a task group but once a month. Search for ways to build knowledge and understanding of one another. This might mean using the first portion of every business meeting to share present life situations with one another. Some organizations have effectively used the idea of breaking the total group up into small sharing groups of three or four to share and commit themselves to pray for each others' needs during the next month. It might mean spending an occasional extended period in a retreat kind of situation. People who know each other communicate much more effectively.

With the rapid pace of changes in society that face us on every hand there never was a greater need to put a major effort into communication. The payoff in increased organizational and individual effectiveness is extremely high!

Books You Might Read

Raymond W. McLaughlin, *Communication for the Church* (Zondervan, 1968), gives a good overall view.

Lyle Schaller's *The Change Agent* (Abingdon) is especially helpful for those who wonder why they can't get other people to follow their lead or take their suggestions.

What's Gone Wrong with the Harvest? by Engel and Norton (Eerdman's) discusses the need for proper understanding of communication as we attempt to communicate the gospel to others. It gives an excellent overview of the communication process.

14.

Making Your Boss Successful

Do you work for an individual or for an organization? Do your subordinates work for you or for your church or agency? Or do they perhaps think they work just for the Lord?

We believe a primary task of each person in his organization is to make his boss successful. If you assumed you went to work for an organization and still work for one, this may seem strange. But it is our conviction that the most effective organizations are those that see themselves as the sum total of their members. Once a person joins an organization, his effectiveness in the organization is dependent on how he relates to his superior, his peers, and his subordinates.

Organizations Are the Result of People

If two people agree to saw a log in half, an organization has been formed. Agreement on a common purpose is assumed. How well they perform or do not perform their task is completely dependent upon how they work together.

If they decide to go into partnership, a more permanent organization has been formed, but its effectiveness will continue to depend on their relationship to each other. Their common purpose remains: cut logs in as efficient a manner as possible.

But perhaps they decide to expand. They subcontract work to other teams. Now the relationship becomes more subtle. However, performance is still easily measurable. The second team's value to the budding company is directly related to how many cut logs they produce.

But let us go further. Success continues to follow their efforts. A sawmill is erected and eventually a lumberyard. Twenty years later there are over 500 employees, including 50 who manage a large tree farm, 47 who work in three lumberyards, a ten-man sales force and 115 people in a sash and door division. "Cutting logs" has now become "supplying finished lumber, sash and doors to the home building industry." What began as a highly relational enterprise has now become diffused. One can now go to work for the tree division of Jones Brothers Inc., or for the sawmill or the sales force. Roles are identified. "I am a millhand." "I am a saleswoman." "I am a manager." Roles and organization become more significant than relationships. Whereas it was rather simple to identify the contribution of the man at the other end of a bucksaw, the contribution of the millwright who keeps all the machines in order is much more difficult to measure.

Nevertheless, regardless of how they think of themselves, the organization is made up of its *people*, and without them it dies.

Organizations Tend toward Bureaucracy

Just as success is often the result of effectiveness, so success tends to breed efficiency. (Not necessarily the same thing!) Job descriptions are written (good). Procedures are defined (good). Policies are formalized (good).

People become more interested in efficiency than effectiveness (bad). As the distance in time and space increases between those who make management decisions and those who carry them out, it becomes more and more difficult for the individual to feel as though he is an integral part of the whole, to believe that he "counts." The day comes when the millhand no longer believes what he does is important. The millwright gets sloppy in oiling the machines. Managers become more interested in their prerogatives than performance, and the organization starts to slide.

Some Assumptions about Organizations

What assumptions are inherent in this scenario?

- Organizations are the result of structural relationships between people.

- Organizations succeed or fail on the strength of these relationships.

- The relationships should be based on assumed common goals, personal motivation, and an ability (skill) to carry out the task (role).

Not so obvious in our narrative was the assumption that the organization has developed standards of both personal and organizational ethics.

Assumptions of the Individual

When he joins the organization the individual also has some assumptions. He assumes:

- The organization can use his abilities.

- He will "get along" with his fellow employees.

- The organization has certain ethical and moral standards and norms (rules) which will be maintained.

A failure of the organization, or the individual, to live up to any of these assumptions, usually leads to a failure of the individual and ultimate separation.

Fitting into the Organization

How often we describe people as "fitting in," either very well or not so well. What we mean is that they view their fellow employees and are viewed by them as doing their assigned job and being emotionally and physically supportive of others.

What makes a person "fit in"? There are obviously many factors: skill, personality, experience. But a great deal depends on whether he or she sees himself as relating to an organization or an individual. We join organizations. We work for and with people.

Making a Success Out of Your Boss

Interpreting and acting on what your superior wants and needs, rather than what you believe the organization wants and needs, have some very practical and important consequences. First, it keeps the lines of responsibility clear. Second, it makes communication much simpler. Third, it keeps loyalties from becoming divided. The result is a much more effective organization and much happier staff members.

Our immediate response to the idea of "my boss first, my organization next" might be, "What if he (she) is a bum? What if he (she) is acting unethically?" That's easy. Get a new boss! "How?" Leave the organization if you have to. But if it is not a question of ethics, then do everything you can to make him (her) effective.

How Do You Make Your Boss a Success?

① *Represent him fairly*. He (she) is also human. He is

bound to have weaknesses and shortcomings. Talk about his abilities and try not to discuss his weaknesses.

② *Try to understand him.* What's his style? People are different. How does he think? *Why* does he think that way? What does he do best? Is he a decision maker, a problem solver, or both?

③ *Try to do it his way,* even if your way seems better. One day he'll discover your way.

④ *Keep him informed.* Don't surprise him. Tell him first ✗ about decisions you want him to make, next what problems you anticipate, and above all what you plan to do.

⑤ *Give him alternatives.* If you are asking for a decision, don't give him an alternative of one. Think through acceptable alternatives. You'll be less disappointed and so will he.

What about "Company Loyalty"?

Haven't military organizations like the Marines done a good job of building *esprit de corps* through "loyalty to the outfit"? What about pride in the organization?

There is little doubt that some organizations have evolved a high degree of pride in their present and past accomplishments and/or methods of operations. But such pride is especially the result of teamwork, and it becomes a spur toward greater cross-commitment rather than a detriment to it.

What about Volunteer Organizations?

Does this apply to the local church? We believe that it does. Too often the local church organization (committee, board, commission) is wrapped up in what it does rather than its goals (Self-Renewal, chapter 11). The volunteer may not describe the group leader in the same terms as his supervisor at work, but his concern for him (her) should be even greater.

Does This Leave Any Room for Criticism?

Personal commitment is a three-way street: up, down, sideways. When we treat others as persons of worth, they usually respond in kind. This in turn produces a climate within which constructive change can take place.

Been working for the organization? Try working for your boss. You may like it.

For Additional Reading

We recommend *Effective Communication on the Job* (Joseph Docher, et al AMA) and Lyle Schaller's *The Change Agent.*

15.

Motivation

"I just don't seem to be able to motivate that man!"
"Why can't people around here be more motivated?"
"People in this church aren't motivated to do anything!"

Sound familiar? Almost everyone recognizes the need to have "highly motivated" people. Few of us seem to know where to find them or how to create them. What is motivation all about anyway? Can you really motivate people? What *is* motivation?

Since we are concerned primarily with leaders within the context of the organizations, we'll limit our discussion to motivation within the organization.

What Is Motivation?

At this stage of our knowledge there is no "one best" theory of motivation, let alone a definition. However, there are some basic ideas that seem to lie behind all the theories proposed. By motivation we usually mean whatever it is inside a person that makes him continue his activity as a human being. We all possess some basic instinctual drives, but these do not by themselves determine our behavior, or even the level of our effort in performance. Rather, how we work out these drives appears to be conditioned by the

123

social environment that surrounds us. The organization within which we work, the culture within which we live, the church within which we worship, all provide guidelines as to what behavior we should choose. This "environment" expects certain things of the individual and rewards him for conforming to its ideals.

The late President Eisenhower is quoted as saying that leadership is "the ability to get people to do what you want because they want to do it." A key concept of management is to "find out what a man wants and make a deal with him." In other words, when we see that motivation is an exchange between the individual and his social environment, we have a key to understanding the meaning of motivation and organization. The organization gives to the individual values and goals within which he can express his drives. When we evaluate whether a person is "motivated" or not, what we are really asking is: Does he meet our expectations as to the kind of behavior we would like to see him have?

Everyone Is Motivated

Everyone is motivated to do something. The key is to bring together within an organization people who are motivated toward the same goals. "Good goals are my goals and bad goals are your goals." If all of the organization's goals are viewed as *our* goals we have made a major step toward motivation.

Why is goal sharing so important? First, it gives us a feeling of doing things we *want* to do. Second, it helps us to believe that we are working on something of value. Third, it makes us feel as though we are *part* of an organization rather than working for "it."

Motivation in the Christian Organization

What might appear at first glance to be a disadvantage

of the Christian organization, namely, its tradition of lower salaries, may in fact be an advantage. It has now been well established by studies that pay is not the *primary* motivator of people. Therefore, the Christian organization will tend to attract people with higher motivation than salary.

However, the local church has probably one of the most complex problems of motivation of any kind of organization in the world. The local church is potentially one of the most sophisticated organizations in the world. First, it is comprised of volunteers. Second, it has two major conflicting purposes: To send people out to do work and at the same time to build them up and nurture them. Third, it accepts into its membership anyone who claims allegiance to its Leader, regardless of his talents, financial condition, or any other qualifications. It is therefore faced with the task of motivating a wide variety of individuals to a wide variety of tasks. (Recognition of this fact will perhaps eliminate the continual failure that most churches experience in trying to get every member involved in any one program.)

Where to Begin

Begin with purposes and goals. It may sound as though we keep continually reemphasizing this subject. We do. We should! The reason so many people come in the front door and soon go out the back door of many Christian organizations, particularly local churches, is that they have either a false or an inadequate conception of what the organization is trying to do. A major task of every administrator when interviewing possible employees should be to clearly spell out the overall goals of the organization and specific objectives with which the employee will be expected to align himself or herself. Since the "new members class" of the local church is performing the same function, a major portion of its time should be used in explaining the purposes and goals of the church and the individual objectives of its members. It follows that a new members class that is not losing, say, approximately 25 percent of those involved is not doing its job. It's just not very likely that *all* of the potential new members will find themselves comfortable with the goals of the organization.

But assuming that we are dealing with individuals who are already members of an organization, what do we do next? Again concentrate on common goals. Bring as many people as possible into the goal-setting process. This does not mean that everyone has to agree on the final decisions, but by setting up a *process*, probably on a yearly basis, in which all members are queried as to what they believe should be the long-range and short-range goals of the organization there will be engendered within the group a feeling of participation. In one survey of individuals' needs within an organization it was discovered that the most highly felt need was to "be in the know" as to what was going on. The organization thus gives goals (values) to its members. At the same time it gives them standards of behavior. If the individual accepts these goals and standards, then he will be motivated to conform to them and perform in a way that will meet the expectations of the group.

What Motivates People?

What are their wants? In *Work and the Nature of Man*, F. Herzberg (Cleveland: World Publishing, 1966), lists extrinsic factors and intrinsic factors.

Extrinsic Factors

1. Pay, or salary increase.
2. Technical supervision or having a competent superior.
3. The human relations quality of supervision.

4. Organization policy and administration.
5. Working conditions or physical surroundings.
6. Job security.

Intrinsic Factors

7. Achievement or completing an important task successfully.
8. Recognition or being singled out for praise.
9. Responsibility for one's own or others' work.
10. Advancement or changing status through promotion.

Using these factors as a general guide, what we might conclude:

1. Pay must be adequate and must also be "fair" since it is often society's direct measure of a person's worth.
2. Do your best never to settle for less than high quality supervision and leadership.
3. View people as a whole. Many times they cannot be motivated positively because they are motivated so negatively in another area of their life.
4. Make your organization's policies clear and the administration of them open and fair.
5. To the best of your ability provide good working conditions.
6. Build security by building competence through training.
7. Keep goals clear and recognize when they have been completed.
8. Always give praise to those responsible for a job well done.
9. Build self-worth by trusting people, by backing them up, and teaching them how to delegate to others.
10. Look for every opportunity to give people more responsibility.

Must Everyone Always Be Motivated?

It is important to see that each individual person must be viewed as a whole. It is fascinating to note the way the men and women in today's society move with apparent ease between their work, recreation, family life, social responsibilities, worship, politics, and a host of other involvements. It is obvious that no one is *highly* motivated to participate in *all* of these activities. This leads to a distinction between what some have called "necessary vs. voluntary behavior." There are a number of things which people will do just because it is "expected of them." Or, another way of thinking about it is that there are things that people will do as part of the price for belonging to an organization. Thus individuals may serve on committees because it is the thing to do, take assignments from their boss because he or she is their boss, or attend social functions about which they feel very little warmth, just to support the group. These are the necessary behaviors. "Voluntary behaviors" are what we do because we want to.

Finding Self-Motivated People

One pastor we know refuses to inaugurate any program within his church unless two things happen; first, it must be suggested by one of the members of the church, and second, a member of the church must volunteer to take responsibility for the program. This pastor has recognized the importance of goal ownership. There is nothing more rewarding than being in charge of *my program*. Another pastor we know has his own private list of goals for his church which he shares with no one. He then encourages those people who seem to have similar goals and fails to encourage people with opposing goals.

It is important to remember here that goals come at all

levels. If you prefer the word "objective" instead of "subgoal," use that, but recognize that many people may be motivated to move just so far with the task and then there will be a need to pass it on to someone else. A person may be motivated to do part of a job, but his motivation may be greatly dampened if he is given a complete job.

One of the best ways of finding motivated people is to let them find themselves. As individuals participate in the goal setting and planning of an organization or of its projects, they will feel a sense of ownership for the goals and the plans. If a large group is used to do the planning, many times potential goal owners will identify themselves by their enthusiasm for what is planned. Look to these people for leadership. They are already motivated.

Maintaining Motivation

Motivation can be increased by giving people opportunities to participate in more things which they feel capable of doing and which they enjoy. At the same time, motivation needs to be maintained. The degree of enthusiasm that the leadership of your organization shows for the project or program in which the individual is involved will have a direct impact on his motivation. List the key people in your organization and then rate yourself against the ten actions that are suggested on page 127. Suggest that the leaders do the same for the people working for them. Your reward will far exceed your investment in time and energy.

16.

You're Fired!''

The situation was not untypical. Jim Roberts had been inwardly seething for the past two months about the performance of the man who was supposed to be his administrative assistant. It seemed that everything Jim gave him to do ended up either late or only 90 percent done. It wasn't that Jim hadn't told him what he wanted done. Somehow over the ten months that Charlie Boyd had worked for Christian Enterprises, Inc., he had never lived up to Jim's original expectation for him. What to do? This was a "Christian" organization! How could Jim get rid of the problem of Charlie Boyd?

Jim had tried to find some "Christian way" of telling Charlie that he was through. But every morning as he headed for the office, knowing that he was going to find another half-done job left over by Charlie, all he could think of saying was, "You're fired!"

How Do You Fire Someone?

There are probably hundreds of Charlie Boyds working for Christian organizations. Maybe right now, as you read this, you know just the person you'd like to really send packing. (Or maybe you have a sneaking feeling that your boss would like to send *you* packing!) How does a Christian organization separate people who are not doing their job? How can they face the problem of "firing"? Whether you are the pastor of a local church or a top executive in a large Christian organization, one day the problem is going to arise.

And how do you handle the problem if the person is a volunteer worker? That one is even harder.

In what follows, we have to first recognize that there are different considerations for different levels of people. We must face up to the fact that our ability to separate people from an organization is directly related to their level of responsibility and *their* investment in the organization.

It's Probably Our Fault

But having said that, the place to start is to first recognize that if there is a need to fire someone, it's usually *our* fault. After all, when a new employee comes to an organization, the person who hires him knows much more about the organization than the prospective employee. The employee is trusting *us* to evaluate his ability to do the job which only we can describe. If you think back on how different your own present job is than what you imagined when you joined your organization, perhaps it will help you to feel what we're saying here.

Preventative Medicine Is Best

So the first step in firing is to do a better job in hiring. Preventative medicine is a lot cheaper than radical surgery.

Write a Job Description

No organization is too small to write a job description

of a position that they want to fill. See chapter 20 for information on how to write one.

Have a Careful Selection Procedure

The next step includes the whole process of selecting a potential employee. With a job description in hand, we then need to gather data about the employee. Again, most organizations probably need some kind of an employment application. (We would think that this would be necessary even for a medium-sized church.) You will find that some companies who produce standard forms will have what you want. Make sure that both professional and personal references are given. *Telephone* the references. Make sure that you are clear in telling them the kind of a job for which you are considering the person.

Don't overlook skills tests. The person may be able to type sixty words per minute, but can he spell? Use the job description as a basis of discussion with the potential employee to make sure that he understands the position for which he is being considered. If it's necessary to compromise, then rewrite the job description on the basis of the job that the person is going to do.

Establish from the beginning that there is going to be a probation period (normally three months), and that at least twice before that time you will review with the employee (again using the job description) their progress in the job. Many jobs take at least a year of on-the-job-experience (this should be in the job description), so the probation period will not always be long enough. But it should be understood from the beginning that such a probation period will exist.

Can You Pay Enough?

We can hear a lot of people saying here, "That's fine,

but we can't be *competitive!*" To a degree this is true. Our experience has been that too often you will get no more than you pay for. If you really can't find a qualified person who can afford to work for what you can pay, we'd recommend you reevaluate your salary structure.

What about Volunteers?

Yes, job descriptions are useful for them, too, as is the evaluation described below. But probably your best safe-guard is to attempt to set an agreed-upon *end date* on every volunteer job. In this way, you can gracefully let the job lapse or change personnel. It makes recruiting easier, too, since the person knows they are not in for life! (See chapter 22.)

Keep Evaluating

Continue to evaluate the employee in a consistent way. Develop a checklist of things you believe are important. Include quality as well as quantity. And ask questions about how they are growing and what would help them grow faster.

Make sure that there are at least semi-annual times when you sit down with the employee and discuss his progress, not only technically against the job description, but his relationship to his fellow employees. Find out what his likes and dislikes are. Many times it's very effective to use an evaluation form in which the employee evaluates himself. (It would be quite appropriate to use the same form you may use.) Time spent in this way will many times help the employee to know, even before you know, that he or she is in the wrong job. As we will see later on, this is the ideal situation. Too often we give undeserved assurances to the employee because we don't want to discourage him, or just because we want to be liked.

People or Task?

There is a continual tension between caring for people and getting the job done. This tension is and should be of particular concern for the Christian organization. It would be un-Christian to work eight to ten hours a day, day after day, with a person and not be concerned about his particular spiritual and social needs. Consequently, it is a good idea to think through the extent to which your organization can enter into the social and emotional support of its employees. Certainly there should be times, however, when the supervisor leaves openings to let the employee communicate some personal needs. There are those times when Christian compassion can only dictate that, for the moment, the job take the back seat to the immediate needs of the individual. We don't have any pat solutions for this, except to indicate that we need to be sensitive in this area.

But Suppose It's Too Late?

Suppose that, for one reason or another, an employee that has been with you for some time is not performing. Some of the preventative steps that we have previously given have not occurred. What do you do now?

Begin by taking responsibility for the situation yourself. Even though the employee may have been transferred from another section or department, you, as the present supervisor, are the one who is immediately responsible.

Isolate the Problem

Next, decide *why* you are dissatisfied with this employee's performance. Is it that not enough work is getting out? Too many errors? Not compatible with fellow employees (the biggest reason for discharging most employees)? Is it the person's attitude? Or are their skills just not adequate? Try to get the emotion out of the situation. If you are burning right at the moment, count to ten and put a date on your calendar when you are going to more calmly consider the problem.

Can You Retrain?

Third, try to envision an improvement or retraining program for this person. Could the individual be given assistance or have some of the work moved to someone else? Are there some procedures which are really at the heart of the entire difficulty? Is it a lack of communication between you and the employee? (How often have you really been together to talk about his job during the last month?)

Where Would This Person Fit?

Fourth, with this analysis in hand, decide what kind of a job situation this person would best fit. This need not be in the same organization. What you are trying to do is to be creative in creating a total life improvement program for the person. Try to think of other organizations who might have this kind of a job, or what kind of additional education or training might be needed.

Set a Termination Date

Fifth, set a termination date based upon the improvements that you think you could make, either temporarily or permanently, in the job situation as it presently stands. Then, with an understanding of how you think this employee could be at his best, make your own trade-off decision on how long you and the organization can wait before this employee is replaced. (And don't forget, while you're thinking about it, that it may be twice as hard to find another person who can do the job as well as this person than it is to retrain or supplement the incumbent.) In your own mind, set a date when you feel the employee must either perform against the needed requirements, or needs to be separated from the organization.

Design a Separation Program

You are now ready to begin a separation program. If there is no job description, begin by discussing with the employee the details of his job, and write a job description with him. Analyze how he is spending his time each day, and look for ways of getting more effective scheduling. Ask the employee to assist you in determining ways of evaluating whether the job is actually being done. You may be surprised at how innovative the person can be in setting up his own measurement standards. Another interesting aspect is that most people set higher standards for themselves than others set for them. End your discussion about the job and its content and evaluation with some specific times when you are going to get back with the employee for review purposes.

Let's assume, for instance, that you are willing to wait for two months before separating the employee. Probably one week after your first discussion you should meet again to just review whether something has been overlooked, and how the individual is feeling about the job description and the evaluation system that has been set up. Then perhaps two weeks later you would have your first real evaluation as to how things are going. This is the time to point out the discrepancies between what you and the employee have agreed is the job, and what is actually being done. Be fair. If things have improved, say so. But where they have deteriorated, indicate that also.

If, after a second review in five weeks, it is obvious in your own mind that things are getting worse rather than better, ask the employee if he can think of another job which he feels that he could be happier at and do better. This may be completely ineffective. The employee may tell you that he loves the job and wants to do it. Here is where the most difficult part comes of trying to get him to see that the very fact that he is not performing against the job is an indication that dissatisfaction is going to increase, rather than decrease. Meanwhile, perhaps you can be thinking of other places in the organization where the employee might work or be scanning the want ads yourself for places for this person.

Do It !

In our theoretical two-month separation program, the sixth week will be key. It is at this point that you have to indicate to the employee that he is either going to be transferred or terminated within the next two weeks. If you have done a good job of preparing him, he may not be surprised. On the other hand, this may evoke a considerable amount of trauma. For a more senior employee, particularly at the executive level, the two weeks may have to be four weeks or six weeks. Again, depending upon the level of the job, you will have to make your own decision as to whether you want to give the employee paid-for time during which he can be looking for another position. (It is always easier to find a job when you have one than when you don't.) Indicate the degree to which you are willing to enter into the problem of finding the better job for the individual, and live up to your word. But set a firm date when termination is going to take place.

What about Long-Term Employees?

The question always arises for the longer-term employee as to whether there should be some severance pay in addition or in lieu of time for job hunting while still in the official employ of the organization. This is the point where your Christian ethics will really have to come into play. If a person has been in your organization for ten years, then you must realize that for the past ten years the organization has been communicating to the employee by its actions that it looks with favor upon his performance. In this case, either the Peter Principle* has gone to work, or the organization has just done a poor job of caring for its people.

Recommendations

Another area of consideration in terms of our business ethics is the degree to which you are willing to write personal letters of recommendation or recommend the person over the telephone. We think that it is important that we be honest here. Think through ahead of time all of the positive things that you are able to say. Be concrete about the negative things also. One thing that is helpful is to ask yourself whether you'd be willing to rehire the employee in another job position if termination is necessary.

Follow-up

Finally, don't overlook the termination interview or perhaps a letter or telephone follow-up two or three weeks after the separation time. After emotions have had a chance to stabilize, you perhaps are more able than any other person to give good counsel and advice as to how this person can improve.

An Exception

Unfortunately, every so often you will hire a person whose morals are such that you cannot afford to have

---

* The "Peter Principle" holds that every person rises through the hierarchy of an organization until he reaches the level of his incompetency. (Perhaps 50 percent true!)

him as part of the organization. Dishonesty or sexual aberrations are the two most common. If you have good evidence that what the employee is doing is illegal, or if it directly impacts on other employees, our opinion would be that you confront him with your evidence and immediately remove him that very day. We are *not* advocating that you kick him out and forget him. To the extent that we can help the individual, we should be ready to do so. We *are* saying, that to leave such a person in the organization after such a confrontation can create havoc with other employees.

Sound Like a Lot of Work?

It is. But suppose the employee were you?

SEPARATION CHECKLIST

_____The job has been described.

_____The employee understands the job.

_____Evaluation criteria have been established.

_____The employee has been evaluated over a long enough period.

_____The employee understands the evaluation.

_____The job cannot be modified to make it possible for the employee to perform satisfactorily.

_____Consideration has been given to other jobs the employee might do.

_____Adequate notice has been given.

_____Job location assistance has been offered where appropriate.

_____A termination interview has been held.

_____Follow-up after termination has been made.

Figure 7

17.

How's Your Delegation

The material in this book is primarily designed for those in Christian organizations. Such organizations differ from secular ones, not only in their goals and purposes, but by their very nature and often in their size and resources. In general, executives in Christian organizations believe they have less personnel available than they need. Some also believe that they must work with people of lower skills and experience. All of this far too often tends to make the Christian executive a poor delegater. But, like his counterpart in the secular organization, the Christian leader cannot do his job unless he delegates.

What Is Delegation?

First of all, delegation is *not* assigning tasks to someone for which he is already responsible. Delegation is assigning to someone else part of *your* job. If you are in an executive position, then your sphere of responsibility greatly exceeds your capacity to do the entire job yourself. Part of your tasks must be delegated.

If you are a pastor of a local church, part of your responsibility is no doubt to deliver a sermon each Sunday morning. From time to time you can ask someone else to do this for you, but usually this is *your* job. However, you can delegate to your secretary, or someone else, part of the research for your sermons, just as you may delegate the typing of the sermon.

If you are an executive in a Christian organization or denomination, you may have responsibility for overseeing a particular aspect of the ministry. You cannot delegate the responsibility for the successful completion of that ministry. However, you can delegate tasks that you would normally do in the fulfillment of that ministry.

Why Are People Confused about Delegation?

Confusion usually exists between what has been delegated and what has been assigned because of the lack of clear lines of authority. Perhaps there is no organization chart, or well-stated yearly and long-range goals. Perhaps the confusion comes because the executive does not understand *how* to delegate.

Steps to Successful Delegation

1. *Decide what needs to be done.* Spell out in your own mind how much responsibility you want to give. In other words, clearly define the task. Perhaps you'll need to write it down, even including some things that it does *not* include.

2. *Select the best person for the job.* This will vary depending on how much time you have to get it done and who is available. If it is an important job, and it needs to be done in a hurry, then it is probably best to select the most capable person. If, on the other hand, it is something that has a fairly low risk due to failure, then perhaps you will want to use the opportunity to delegate as a means of training someone else.

3. *Make the assignment clear.* Many times, because a

person has been working closely with you, a simple "Will you do this?" is adequate. However, if the task is somewhat unfamiliar to the delegate, then make sure that he fully understands everything that is expected of him. Sometimes it is important to tell him why *he* was selected in order that he can see the importance of the task to himself and to the organization.

4. *Establish level of authority.* Perhaps more confusion is created here than in any other aspect of delegation. There are a number of levels of delegation:

- Do it and don't report back.

- Do it and report back immediately.

- Do it and report back routinely.

- Investigate and make recommendations to me, and I will decide.

5. *Anticipate the problems.* Make sure that others with whom the delegate will be working understand his task and his responsibility. Tell him about the others with whom he will be working and clear the way for him if needed. Tell him about past experiences with this kind of assignment and difficulties you may have experienced yourself. Make sure that he knows how to get to you if he needs additional help.

6. *Build in checkpoints.* Work out during the time of the assignment dates or times when you will get together to compare notes and check on progress. Make certain the delegate knows the type of reports you want and whether you will be following up informally or formally.

7. *Evaluate and build on results.* Both you and the person to whom you delegate can learn a lot from the assignment. If it was other than a routine task you may

then want to give special appreciation. If things didn't turn out quite as you expected, then you should analyze where the difficulty lay.

When Should You Delegate?

Obviously you should delegate as many of the routine tasks as you possibly can. Screening your mail, handling routine correspondence, and a number of other such assignments can be delegated to your secretary. (See chapter 23.)

Another obvious category of things to delegate are those for which you don't have time yourself. This may be due to either some unexpected circumstances or just increased responsibilities on your part. They may be things that you would like to do if you had the time. They may even be things which you do very well, but because of the situation you face must take a lower priority.

Many times they will be part of your own work in which others have special skills, perhaps greater than yours! Researching a particular situation for background data for a report, designing a program or meeting, handling the technical side of a negotiation with a supplier or sister organization are all examples of situations in which delegation may be appropriate because someone else can do it better.

As your own job responsibilities grow, you have to delegate more and more. Many times you will actually be making full-time *assignments*, rather than just delegating; you may actually have to break off a piece of your work and give it to someone else to do.

High priority items—don't delegate; low priority items—delegate.

When Not to Delegate?

You can't delegate responsibility for *your job*.

Don't delegate policy items, decisions which affect the overall operation of your organization.

Don't delegate if you're the only person who knows how to do the job. If the job is of such a nature, technical or otherwise, that only you can do it, passing it on to someone else is an exercise in futility.

Don't delegate your responsibility for your own people and their personal needs.

Don't delegate to pass the buck. Sticky situations will arise. Handle them yourself.

The Benefits of Delegation

Delegation frees you up for higher priority items.

Delegation gives other people experience and helps you to assess their capability.

Delegation many times can be a challenge and give people a sense of participation in what's going on.

The Pitfalls of Delegation

People assume that they have more authority than you have given them, and as they fail to report back, you lose control.

Other people will never do things exactly the same way that you would, and this will cause anxieties on your part. The thing that you delegate may get in the way of some other priority items that the delegate is already working on.

Why Don't We Delegate More?

Probably because we are so busy worrying about today that we haven't been building for tomorrow. We are afraid that if we let go of something right now, it will not be done properly, and so we try to hang on to everything and only drive ourselves at a higher and more demanding pace.

Many times we overlook the magnitude of the task we have undertaken for ourselves for our organization and don't realize that we cannot do it all single-handedly.

Special Problems for the Christian Organization

There are two special problems with which many executives in Christian organizations have to deal. The first of these is the use of volunteer workers. When you delegate part of your work to a volunteer it is especially important that you make sure: (1) you believe that he can do the job, (2) you have a clear understanding as to when he is going to report back to you, and (3) you have all the backup assistance that you or he may need. By carefully spelling out what is to be delegated and checking with the delegate to be sure that he has both the time and the know-how to do the job, much of this problem can be overcome.

A second, and less obvious problem, results from that which is usually a major advantage of the Christian organization—its sense of common purpose and direction. Many times your subordinates believe that they "know what's best for the organization" and instead of seeing the task that you have delegated to them as coming from you will see it as part of the *organization's* task. With such a perception, their feedback to you and communication to you about what they are doing can easily break down. Again, this kind of problem can best be handled by clearly spelling out ahead of time what is to be done and what are the checking points along the way.

How to Begin

If you believe that you have not been doing a very good job of delegating, and would like to do better, start by making the list of all of the items which you believe you could delegate.

Next, analyze the kinds of people to whom you could delegate them. Then write clear statements of what it is you want to have done. Contact your potential delegates and see whether they are willing and able to take on your delegation. Make a list of those items which you have delegated and the dates on which you are going to follow up either formally or informally. Maintain a private "delegation performance chart." This will enable you to sort out those people with whom you are having the greatest success delegating and also will point out to you delegations that are "boomeranging" or not working out the way you expected them to.

18.

Decision-Making

Many years ago a Christian leader wrote a letter to some of his followers in Corinth reflecting back on his decision not to visit them: "Was I vacillating when I wanted to do this? Do I make my plans like a worldly man, ready to say Yes and No at once? As surely as God is faithful, our word to you has not been Yes and No. For the Son of God, Jesus Christ, whom we preached among you, Silvanus and Timothy and I, was not Yes and No; but in him it is always Yes" (2 Cor. 1:17-19).

Paul faced all the demands for making a decision. The situation *demanded action*. He was under a *time pressure*. He *lacked complete information*. There was *uncertainty* which suggested a risk in making a decision. There were possible *costly consequences* if he made the wrong decision. On the other hand, there was the possibility of *good benefits* from an effective decision. Last, there was the possibility of *two or more alternative actions*.

The need for a decision comes at any time of the day, and decisions come in all sizes:

"We have chairs in the aisle at our Sunday morning service. What should we do?"

"Mr. Jones' wife is having her first baby, and they want you at the hospital in the next half-hour . . ."

"The XYZ organization wants us to loan Bill Williams to them for six months for a special project. Can he go?"

"People are spilling coffee on the new rug in the Green Room. What should we do?"

"We have just received a $20,000 bequest from Robert Jordan's will. What should we do with it?"

"The Fire Department inspector says we either have to stop using this building or spend $28,000 on a sprinkler system. What shall we do?"

"Who will . . . how can we . . . ?"

Good decision-making is the hallmark of effective leadership in an organization. But good decision-making in Christian organizations requires an additional dimension. It is this additional spiritual dimension that can give the Christian executive the confidence he needs to move ahead with a decision while others stand and vacillate.

The Elements of Decision-Making

There is a close relationship between decision-making and problem-solving. Usually both start with a statement like, *"Something* needs to be done!" The steps in the process are not difficult to describe:

- *Identify and describe the situation.* Gather as many relative facts together as possible.

- *Line up alternatives.* These may range from taking no action (a decision in itself), to a number of possible actions.

- *Compare the various alternatives* against each other. There will usually be advantages and disadvantages to each.

- *Calculate the risk of each.* Since you usually will not have enough information to make the decision, face up to the possible consequences of each alternative.

- *Select the best alternative.* If alternatives have been adequately compared and rated as to risk, many times the best one will be self-evident.

Your first reaction may be that anything that complicated just isn't useful. But like so many things our mind is able to comprehend and digest in a brief moment, the *process* by which comprehension occurred takes a little longer to describe. So let us press on.

Describing the Situation

Good managers know that many times just their ability to understand a situation is half of the solution. Gather as many facts as possible. There will never be enough, but within the time demands of the decision take time to organize the data that *is* available. Data gathering is a skill that needs to be developed. What are the key sources of information? Whom should you call in? But remember at this point you're asking for data, not opinions or what decision should be made.

Line Up Alternatives

From the data that you have gathered, list possible alternatives in some way that will permit you to visualize them at one time. If you are working with a group, it is very helpful to write the data (problem description) on one piece of newsprint and then to list the alternatives on another.

There will be cases when a decision is either yes or no, go or don't go. However, try not to be satisfied with only two alternatives. Get wise counsel. Ask other people for possible alternatives based upon the data that you have.

Compare the Alternatives

Since we can never completely predict the future, almost every alternative will include some factor of uncertainty. Find some way to compare alternatives one against the other. Some of the things that you might want to compare are the *risk* involved (see below), the *cost* of the alternative, the *people available* to implement the decision, the *past effectiveness* of using this type of alternative, the *amount of time* that this alternative will require and *how it will be received* within the organization.

A *list of assumptions* that you are making for each one of the alternatives may be a key to which is the best. It is surprising how often people arrive at the same conclusion for different reasons. Therefore, a side benefit of listing your assumptions is your ability to communicate to others (and yourself) the base upon which you are building your reasoning.

How much time you take in this process will, of course, be dictated by the urgency of the decision you face.

Calculate the Risk

The major difference between problem-solving and decision-making is that in problem-solving we assume that there is a right solution. The problem *has* an answer. But decision-making almost always includes an element of risk. We *don't* have enough information. We are not sure of the future. We don't have enough time to gather all the data. Therefore, try to develop your own method of rating the risk of each of the alternatives. Perhaps something as simple as a grading scale of one to ten will be of help. Look back at your previous assumptions and see if they help you in assessing the penalties for making the wrong decision.

Many times the correct alternative is self-evident as we compare and rate the risk of each one of the various alternatives. But there are many times when it is very difficult to choose between alternatives. What do we do now?

Sometimes you can combine alternatives. This can be done by taking parts of two different alternatives or perhaps trying both of them. For instance, one might be a short-range solution to the need that you face while the other might be a longer range solution. Don't be afraid of a compromise. Inflexibility in decision-making tends to destroy effective leadership. Often all you can do is make the best out of a series of bad situations. But intuition or hunches will play a major role in selecting the "best" alternative. Here is where the spiritual dimension really matters. Pray about the alternatives. Seek God's promised wisdom.

Implement the Decision

How a leadership decision is announced and implemented many times is just as important as the decision itself. If it will have a major impact on the life of the organization, consider the *timing* of the announcement. Perhaps it should be postponed until just the right set of circumstances present themselves. When you make an important decision, take a little time before announcing it. Sleep on it. God may have other plans!

The *manner* in which the decision is announced is of tremendous importance. If it is presented as "I'm sorry, fellow, but this is the best we can do in this lousy situation . . ." then you can expect the same response in your subordinates as they communicate the decision throughout the organization.

153

The *individuals* to whom the decision is announced can make a big difference in its reception. Many times it is a good idea to privately lay some groundwork ahead of time with those who are going to have to implement or be affected by a major decision.

Once a decision is made, don't look back or second-guess yourself. Expect and demand commitment to the decision on your part and on the part of those who are going to be working on it. Don't seek popularity in decision making. Leadership can be a lonely business. Be consistent in applying the consequences of your decision. Don't vacillate.

When Things Go Wrong

As every veteran leader knows, "If there is a possibility of anything going wrong, it probably will." What may have been a very good decision three weeks ago, in the light of subsequent events or new data, may now appear to be a very poor one. This means that important decisions should have a built-in feedback process which will let you know as soon as possible things are going sour. At this point, it is not a question of who's at fault, but how to turn things in a more positive direction. In a sense, you are faced with a new decision: what to do with the bad one you've made! It may be that the decision was right, but the planning was poor. Perhaps the wrong individuals were given the assignment to implement. Perhaps a new and better alternative has appeared, one which is distracting people from the original course of action. Go through the same process of decision-making that you went through before: identify the situation, line up alternatives, compare alternatives, calculate the risk, select the best new alternative, implement a new and revised decision.

It is here that the Christian executive has the tremendous

advantage over his secular counterpart. Each one of us as sons of God can be assured that God is working all things together for good on our behalf. But those of us who are privileged to work as part of the organizational life of his body have the right to assume that this applies equally to the organizational task. This does not mean that we should be casting blame for failure on the Lord. Nor should we discount our own role in any "successes." It does mean that that extra dimension can produce decisions that can turn the world upside down.

Some Books That Can Help

Lyle E. Schaller has recently authored *The Decision-Makers: How to Improve the Quality of Decision Making in the Churches* (Abingdon).

A standard work that has been used in a number of Christian organizations is *The Rational Manager: A Systematic Approach to Problem Solving and Decision Making*, by Kepner and Tregoe (McGraw-Hill).

19.

...A Word of Appreciation

Christian leaders are the object of a great deal of appreciation, and we need all we can get! Of course, appreciation can become an insulating kind of security blanket. Most leaders attain greater responsibility and recognition because they *are* appreciated, and as they move "upward" they tend to gather around them those who appreciate them the most. After all, none of us *likes* negative criticism. It is all too easy to hear only what we like to hear. We respond the most to those who respond to us.

But what about the people we lead? Are they feeling those same pleasant vibrations? Do the people who work closest to us know us as that warm, friendly personality we wear before the Christian public?

Some of us are by nature "relational" people. If we err in one direction it's spending too much time with people and not enough time on tasks. In fact, our current position may be the result of that kind of leadership. But there are others of us who become so involved in "the work" that we forget the people. That desperately needed word of appreciation is seldom heard on our lips.

Why Do We Need to Be Appreciated?

That may seem like a silly question, but let's stop a minute to see the different levels involved. First I need to be *recognized as a person*. During these hours we share together in organizational life I want to be seen and understood as something more than an employee or a staff member. I live and move and have my being in a larger world. Second, I need assurance that *what I am doing is worthwhile*. If this is a *Christian* work, it must be part of a larger whole (mustn't it?). Where do I fit? Third, I want to believe that I am *doing a good job*. The primary way I come to believe these things is through the appreciation of others, particularly "significant others."

Doing Tasks vs. Loving People

There is a tension here. Nowhere else is it greater than in a local church, for the local church is dedicated to two conflicting purposes: *caring* for its members and *sending* them forth to do the work of Christ. But the glue that holds any organization together is loving communication and the communication of love. Love is acts. It takes work. There is a "get-readiness" to many acts of love that is too often overlooked. That spontaneous expression of appreciation is often the result of a great deal of preparation and practice.

Initiation and Response

Love responds. Love also initiates. There are acts you can initiate as a leader and actions you can take as an organization. There are also responses you can be prepared to make. Let's look at initiations and responses for both the individual and the organization.

Personal Initiative

Most of us need to develop a discipline of periodically reviewing our performance in expressing appreciation.

There are a number of milestones or events that can be used as triggers. Some of these are readily available. Others you will have to work at. Birthdays are obvious. But what about a person's organization anniversary date, wedding anniversary, even their spouse's birthday? A card, of course. But a personal note to home or office desk, sometimes a small gift, a surprise coffee-break party—all indicate that you took some extra time to care.

Do you ever take your subordinates out to lunch just to be with them—no business, no objective, just to be available and listening? Try it. You'll like it.

Do people *see* you? If you are out of the office quite a bit or holed up in meetings, just walking through the entire office and touching people with a word or a smile or a hand on the shoulder, lets them know you want to be available.

Do people see *you?* We wear many different hats and play many different roles. Do the people who work for you only see you wearing your cloak of leadership? Do you give opportunity to your staff for them to say they appreciate you?

If these suggestions seem a bit calculated or contrived, think of them only as entry points, certainly not ends in themselves.

Personal Response

Don't be afraid of saying, "Thank you" for a job well done. It can't be said too often. It can be expressed in many ways—a note or memo, a scribbled "great job" across a report, a phone call, a public compliment in a staff meeting.

Be ready to listen. Our greatest gift is ourself. You may not be able to solve the problem, to heal the hurt, to correct the wrong, but the fact that you have taken the time to understand and to feel says that you consider both the need and the person important. "Yes. I *hear* you."

And when the time comes for a rebuke or reprimand, make sure it is preceded by an expression of appreciation for the good things done. And never do it in the presence of others.

Don't forget that your subordinate's failure is primarily *your* failure. You probably were responsible for training him. You are responsible for tracking his performance well enough to see him through the troubled waters.

A compliment to a subordinate or peer is five times more effective than a reprimand. At the same time, don't gloss over failure. Success is only meaningful if we can distinguish it from failure.

Organizational Initiatives

If an *organization* is going to communicate appreciation to an individual, it must be done on the basis of his or her expectations. Too often organizations (both Christian and secular) assume that the employee has a clear picture of what is expected of him, or, if he does not, that he can develop it on his own. The result is a considerable divergence between what the employee believes the organization wants and what his supervisor really wants from him or her. Perhaps you never thought of it this way, but a job description is the foundation of *overall* appreciation. It's great to be complimented for the individual task, but ultimately each of us wants to hear how we are doing in our total role.

This means that a time of regular personal evaluation is a must. The positive results of such evaluation can be expressed in many ways: promotion, training opportunities, public recognition.

When the opportunity for a new assignment comes

along, use the occasion to tell the person about the good attributes that qualified him or her for the job.

But individuals can also be appreciated as part of a group. The organization can provide fellowship times in daily group devotions, corporate meetings, department retreat days, luncheons or dinners. And don't overlook means of telling people what's going on in the organization. Use meetings, newsletters, announcements. Communicate!

All of these are indications that investment of time and money in *staff* people is considered worthwhile. People *are* important.

Organizational Response

In a day when the complexities of Western life threaten to overwhelm us, it seems obvious that we need to be prepared to respond to illness, death, and personal tragedy. Health insurance, life insurance, and accident insurance programs are ways to help the individual cope with society. So are vacations and sick leave as well as optional time away such as a birthday bonus day.

There Are No Unimportant People

Pious words. Hopefully more than that. The secular organization recognizes that it has a bigger investment in its president than in a newly hired clerk and acts accordingly. There is a basic principle of organizational survival here that needs to be recognized. Top leaders *do* need more freedom and flexibility. Rules that were designed for the eight-to-fiver just don't fit a person whose job requires him to arrange his or her life according to organizational needs. But the "prerogatives of leadership" are easily misunderstood, both by those on whom they are bestowed and by those who sit in the spectator's seat.

For there are also "prerogatives of followership," and those prerogatives include recognition of persons and appreciation of what they are and what they are doing. The grace of appreciation is too often missing in the Christian organization.

It's Not Easy

Human nature gets in the act, both our own and others. What was a pleasant surprise last year becomes expected this year. Patterns of appreciation are soon recognized, and the *failure* to act begins to convey more meaning than the act itself. We never arrive. The message of love has to be framed in new words and different actions. If you are already doing all the things we have suggested, you have an even bigger challenge.

If you are doing very few, begin today. You may be surprised at how appreciative you can become.

APPRECIATION CHECKLIST

_____I have written a personal note of appreciation to a staff member this week.

_____I usually remember people's birthdays.

_____I know how long each person reporting to me has been with the organization.

_____I have discussed a *personal* problem with a staff member in the last two weeks.

_____I discuss personal performances with each of my staff members at least once a year.

_____I have thought about and have goals for the personal growth of those reporting to me.

_____I have had lunch with a member of my staff in the last week.

_____Our organization is continuously analyzing cost-of-living against present salaries.

_____We supply training opportunities to qualified staff.

Figure 8

PART THREE

Leadership Tools

20.

Job Descriptions

In chapter 10 we discussed the concept of management by objectives as being a very effective approach to managing the Christian organization. What particularly commends it is the emphasis on purpose and goals, rather than on organizational or functional structures. It has the further advantage of providing a means of evaluating the individual performance.

There will be those Christians who draw back from the edge of personal evaluation. It is one thing to talk about our organizational failures or successes. It is quite another to discuss individual performance. But to the contrary, should it not be in the very nature of a Christian organization that we be open enough to one another to seek an understanding of where we are contributing and where we are hindering organizational effectiveness?

But it is a difficult task at best. One excellent way to carry it out is on the basis of a position, or job description.

What Is a Job Description?

Basically, a job description is a written outline of what is expected of an individual in a particular job. It is a description of the job, not the person filling it. It centers on

167

what is to be accomplished, rather than who is to accomplish it.

What Is It Good For?

It not only helps the organization and the individual measure his performance against goals, but it has a number of other uses, depending on the type and size of the organization.

For the larger organization with a scaled salary structure, job descriptions not only help us compare one job with another inside the organization, but also to more accurately compare our pay scales with others'. For the latter this is about the only way to keep from comparing apples with oranges. It is especially true for jobs with generic titles such as "secretary." Such a title can cover anyone from a typist to a member of a board. A job description gives it definition.

A job description is perhaps most valuable when there is a need to fill a new or a vacant position. It clarifies what kind of a person to seek. It gives the potential staff member a picture of what is expected of him or her. Remember the person hiring has the greater responsibility. If the new employee doesn't succeed, it's probably your fault. (See "You're Fired!" chapter 16.)

A job description helps relate one job to another. It not only should place any necessary boundaries around a job, but also help the incumbent to see his job as part of a larger whole.

What Should It Contain?

Date—They get obsolete quickly!

Title—Try to be descriptive without being too wordy. If there are a number of grades in the job, consider a

standard set of terminology: junior secretary, intermediate secretary, senior secretary.

Purpose—Describe the *why* of the job. What is supposed to be accomplished because this job exists! "In
order to . . ." This is the place to fit in the general and perhaps the spiritual aspects of the job.

Type of Supervision—Either a statement as to what position (not person) this job reports or, for a larger organization, one of a category of types of supervision such as
general, regular, close, the employee will be under.

Responsibility—Without going into a great deal of detail, be as specific as possible. Not "acts as a secretary,"
but "takes machine dictation, transcribes letters, reports
and other documents using an electric typewriter. Sets up
and operates an office filing system, etc."

Include a statement about the amount of supervision
exercised and how detailed this supervision must be—
"Gives close supervision to a secretary and two clerks."

Don't try to cover everything. If you have described
75–90 percent of the job, that's adequate.

It always is a good idea to have an ending paragraph—
"Performs other duties as requested." This will cover
anything you have missed and may save a lot of misunderstanding later.

Education and Experience—These are grouped together
because they complement each other so closely. A rule
of thumb is that two years' experience equals one year of
education. Give the minimum amount and the type of
education needed *to do the job.*

Then give the minimum and normal maximum years and
type of experience. For example, four to six years' experience, including two years as an associate pastor."

Last, include a statement about the amount of *on-the-*

job experience that will be expected in *this* job before the job is being completely filled. No one can do a job adequately on the first day they arrive, and many executive jobs are only fully comprehended after one to two years' experience.

Working Conditions—Where will the job be carried out? Does it require any unusual hours? Is travel required? If so, how many days per month away will be required? Are there any other unusual features to the job, such as a good deal of driving?

Special Requirements—Are there any special licenses or peculiar skills required, such as preaching license, flying or driver's license?

What Not to Include

Don't include factors that relate to the *person* rather than the job—salary, vacation, sick leave, etc. These should be covered in a general organizational policy and any deviations from policy negotiated with the individual.

Using a Job Description for Evaluation

A few job descriptions can be so specific that it is possible to tell immediately whether the incumbent is performing above or below the standard set. But most will require the establishment of individual plans with personal milestones.

In a local church, the duties of the pastoral staff may be very broad. They may be such that to emphasize one may require the de-emphasis of another. This is why each staff member, working with the responsible board or individual, should write out the specifics of what is to be accomplished each year and how it will be measured. This may be in the form of a particular accomplishment (institute an adult

Bible class) or a number of events (make ten home visits each month).

But whether in a local church or other organization, review and evaluation should not be limited to once a year. Preferably there should be a quarterly discussion about performance against goals. They may need to be changed! No job is a static thing. New situations will demand a new focus. Just make sure you don't let yourself off the hook by changing the requirements *after* the job is done. Remember anyone can hit the bull's-eye if you draw the target after the shot is fired. The job description should be seen as the boundary within which all milestones and goals should be found.

How to Begin

In an organization of more than a few people, introduce the program with care and thoughtfulness. It may be viewed as an attempt to check up on people's performance rather than to benefit the entire group. Call a meeting to explain the time schedule and what is expected. Show how the final product will be used. Emphasize that you are after information about the *job*, not the person.

Using the outline given above, ask each person to describe *their job*, not themselves. Have the supervisor either write a parallel description or review the one submitted by the staff member. The supervisor and staffer should then do their best to reconcile any differences.

If you are encountering difficulty obtaining a description, go to the interview approach. Here make sure you avoid "why" questions and concentrate on how, what, and where.

In a larger organization, you may want to first establish the meaning of some standard terminology, such as levels (junior, intermediate, senior), levels of supervision (close, regular, general, broad), or equivalents (one year of education is equivalent to two years of experience).

Try to use a standard format so that each job is seen in relation to the others.

Write descriptions for all levels, every job.

Don't overlook the tremendous benefit of job descriptions for *volunteer staff*. (See chapter 22.)

Some Warnings

Writing job descriptions takes time and effort. Don't start without planning enough hours to do an adequate job. If you are going to do an entire organization, plan on at least six months to complete the job.

Job descriptions get out of date quickly. Make it a yearly practice to have each employee and supervisor review and rewrite each year.

Don't let the job description get in the way of doing the job. It's a beginning point. Be ready to change it.

If you are planning to use the job description to establish salary scales, you may want outside professional help.

Some Additional Advantages

One consulting firm that we know analyzes the communication within an organization by asking each person to describe his or her job and then asking the supervisor to describe the same job. The theory is that if there is a good communication up and down, there will be a close match between the two descriptions. Written job descriptions can be used for the same type of analysis. Many men and women who are frustrated by their inability to please their superior, along with many superiors who are frustrated with those who are working for them, are quite surprised to discover what the other really thought the job amounted to. By *limiting* areas of responsibility many times the incumbent is greatly relieved, while at the same time, a discussion between subordinate and superior may provoke a statement like, "I never realized you wanted me to do *that!*" A broader job description may then be necessary.

It follows that job descriptions are an excellent vehicle for delegating tasks and at the same time pointing out to the superior his or her failure to delegate.

Many times the writing of a series of job descriptions will identify holes in the organization—work that everyone thought someone else was doing. At the same time, they may uncover duplication and overlap of effort.

A Top Management Responsibility

The details of the job description program may be delegated to those outside the top management level of the organization. But whether it is the board of a local church or the management of a large service agency, time should be set aside for a critical review of the finished product and a discussion as to whether these descriptions do adequately fit into the goals and purposes of the organization.

21.

Filing

There are few people who enjoy filing and even fewer who enjoy trying to find something they have filed. But since our culture is based upon the written word, most of us put up with the need for filing as graciously as possible.

What's the Purpose?

If more of us would ask that simple question, "Why?" we probably would do many things differently. What's the "Why?" of a filing system?

The fundamental purpose of a filing system is to *retrieve* something, not to store it.

If we start with that basic understanding, we will save ourselves a great deal of frustration at both ends of the system. How is your filing system arranged? Chances are that you have some sort of an alphabetical system which is arranged by subject, or perhaps by the name of the individual who is corresponding with you or with your organization. You are trapped already! You have filed things in a way that may seem easy to store them, but is very difficult to retrieve.

Think for a moment *why* you want to retrieve some of the information that you have filed. Perhaps you need it to refer back to a previous letter when writing to someone. If you are a pastor, perhaps you need information for future sermons. If you are an executive in a Christian organization, you probably need information about projects on which you are working, minutes of the last meeting you attended, or information about a particular area of your operation so that you can prepare for the next step.

The next question to ask yourself is, How valuable is the information and what will happen if I cannot retrieve it?

A fundamental law of all filing systems is that the faster you can file it, the longer it will take to retrieve it. Expressed in another way: the cost of retrieving something will be inversely proportional to the cost of storing it. If you spent very little time and money filing it, you will probably spend a great deal of time and money retrieving it. You, as an executive, have to decide where you want to make your investment in time and money. This is *fundamental* to the design of all filing systems.

From Informal to Formal

Once we get the idea that filing systems are for the purpose of *retrieving* things, we'll see that there are all kinds of systems available to us.

Many executives have found that just by carrying a secretary's spiral notebook to all of their meetings, they can jot down in random form any "to do" items that may come up. When the telephone rings they reach for the same notebook to jot down information that they expect to receive. Before they make a phone call, they note the name of the person they're calling and his phone number (in case they miss him this time) and then make notes on the conversation. In this way they can capture at no additional time and expense information that they may need in the future, even though they are not sure at this time that they will. A daily review of the notebook will transfer the information into more formal channels.

Make It Come Back to You

A filing system should be designed whenever possible so it "automatically" gives you the information you want. Most information is related to some date. By jotting a note on pieces of correspondence or documents that pass over your desk as to a date when you would like to see it again, it can be put into a pending file. Some member of your staff can go through the file on a daily basis and return to you the document that you wanted on the requested date. This is useful as a follow-up device for other people with whom you may be working. You can use it to follow up on yourself. A note written to yourself about a pending meeting will remind you to prepare for it.

Plan Ahead

A somewhat more formal, and still time-oriented, filing system is one which sets up folders against planned events. For the pastor these would obviously include sermons. By sketching out sermon titles, say for the next twenty-six weeks, and setting up a folder for each, the pastor can store illustration material, reference material, or other things that come his way in an appropriate folder, knowing that someday the sermon will come up. For both the pastor and Christian executives, having folders for the next series of meetings is a real help. Correspondence that refers to a forthcoming meeting or data that you might receive between meetings can be put into the appropriate folder. The dates across the top of the folder along with the subjects are a reminder of what lies ahead. When the time for the meeting comes, you can pull the folder and take it with you. Minutes from previous meetings can be kept in the same folder and the folder just moved up into the time of the next meeting. The same system is also very useful in planning trips.

It is obvious that this kind of a filing system reflects the way we actually do our work rather than some abstract system.

Filing Correspondence

But what about the voluminous correspondence that may come to us from individuals in all walks of life? The rule is the same: The more it costs to file it, the cheaper it will be to retrieve it.

When filing information from a variety of sources there is a great tendency to arrange it alphabetically. However, there are many problems with this approach, particularly when filing correspondence.

First, it is extremely difficult to file alphabetically, particularly by the names of individuals. The chances of error are very high. Consequently if you keep all of the correspondence listed under A, B, or C, there is a good possibility that some of the correspondence will be "lost."

Second, if you elect to set up a separate folder for each of your correspondents, you will soon have a file drawer full of folders. Unless you know that you're going to carry on a lengthy correspondence with an individual, you have set up a file folder that may never be used again.

Third, alphabetical files are very difficult to purge. File drawers and floor space for file cabinets are both expensive. If you recognize this, and want to go through a yearly cleaning out, you'll either have to throw out the folders or go through the entire process of reviewing everything that's in file.

Where, Not What

The best way to file things is not by *what* they are but *where* they are. Instead of locating documents or correspondence by the name of the writer or the subject, consider assigning a document number to each letter or document. This might have a prefix for the year it was filed, followed by the next sequential number. This will overcome one of the first objections to alphabetical filing; filing accuracy will go up.

But how do you find it? Obviously the file number is going to have to be kept in some way that is useful to you. For correspondence, we suggest a daily log in which the name, date, and perhaps the subject of the letter are noted. This is followed by the next sequential document number. We further suggest that you keep a 4-by-6 or 3-by-5-inch card with the name and address of the correspondent and the numbers of the documents which refer to him in some way. (He either wrote it, received it, or received a copy.) This means that you have two ways to find the document. If you can remember the approximate date on which it was written, or if you can remember the name of the person to whom it was written or by whom it was written, you can find the document.

"But," you say, "suppose I want to get all of the letters from Jim Brown? Isn't this going to take a lot of time and trouble?" You'll be surprised at how quickly you can go through a numerical file and pull seven or eight letters. And you'll also be pleased with how quickly you can refile them using a numerical system.

You can also carry this system a great deal further. For you can set up a set of subject cards on which you place the numbers of any documents that refer to that subject. In other words, one document with only one number can be listed in as many places as you choose. This is particularly advantageous if there are any number of copies that are sent to different individuals within the same organization, or if you send out one general letter to a number of people. By posting the number of only one document on each address card, you have covered all contingencies with only one piece of paper in file.

We suggest that if you use a numerical filing system you use hanging file folders and keep 100 document numbers to a folder.

Note some further advantages of this system. It is *easy to purge* because you can tell by the number of the documents how old they are, and you can discard older ones if you care to.

It is easy to microfilm; in fact, it is about the only practical way. Because documents are in sequential order, rather than in subject order, you can easily put them on a microfiche or microspool and quickly locate them using the indexing system that you have devised.

General Organizational System

When we set up filing systems for our personal use, we do so with the idea that if they don't work we can probably change them. It's not quite that simple for organizations. Changing the filing system for an organization is a major undertaking. Therefore, it is worthwhile to get competent counsel, both at the time of installing an organizational filing system or at the time of evaluating the one you have. Moving paper around is an extremely costly business. Expenditure at the planning end of the line will save a lot of misery at the other end. Try to project your organization three to five years into the future. What will it be doing then? What will its needs be? What kind of data will you as a Christian executive want to be able to recall so that you can make more effective decisions in the future? How many documents will you have? How many correspondents? This will take you away from the mundane questions of filing systems into the overall need for a management information system.

Make sure that whatever system you use is one that's tailored to your needs. There are many time-saving mechanical devices on the market from special card holders to microfilm systems. However, don't be sold on gadgets. Look for performance.

What about Computers?

Computerized filing has two major advantages. It can store and retrieve *large* amounts of data at a low cost, and it can rearrange or select data at a much lower cost than doing a large amount manually. At World Vision we have a sophisticated name handling system and receipting system that can perform a wide range of services. We also store and retrieve a great deal of research information in computerized files. But although the cost savings is potentially large if the volume is high enough, the risks are not small.

Our advice would again be to get the best counsel you can. Select a system that will meet most of your needs now and hopefully will be expandable. Don't expect miracles. Good computerized information systems are the results of good, *hard* work.

Don't Forget File 13

When all is said and done, most of us have to admit there is a great deal of information we keep that we never look at again. Probably a good rule for filing would be "When in doubt, don't."

22.

Volunteers

The members of the body of Christ are mostly volunteers: people who are (1) not paid for their work, (2) who know that they don't *have to* do the job for a living, and (3) can therefore quit anytime. How many volunteers a Christian organization can use will vary. The local church is made up predominantly of volunteers. A Christian mission agency, on the other hand, will have a minority of people who are volunteers in the above sense.

This is a day in which the local church seems to have more and more difficulty in recruiting and maintaining people in assigned tasks. Meanwhile the para-church organizations are having greater need for assistance. An analysis of how to recruit, train, lead and fulfill a group of people as volunteers would seem very much in order. Because the majority of volunteers work in local churches, we will concentrate our discussion here. But much of what is discussed is applicable to any volunteer organization.

The Situation

It is a sad fact of life that most individuals who work in a volunteer capacity in the local church for any length of time come away from the experience debilitated rather than inspired. The amount of job satisfaction that they receive seems to be inversely proportional to the size of the church. If they are key people in a small church, then they may have very good feelings of self-esteem and feel that they are making a real contribution. However, if they are one of many individuals in the large church with many different committees, there is a great tendency for them to feel like they are just part of the machinery.

This is particularly true of churches with large paid staffs. As such staffs begin to multiply and a team spirit develops within them, there is an increasing tendency to make decisions for the members (volunteers) of the church and decide not only *how* they should do the work, but what work they should do. The result is many laymen within the church who feel like objects of somebody else's program rather than lay *leaders* of their church.

Meanwhile, we continually encounter the situation where the pastor and the rest of the staff are overworked and the lay people are undertrained. Pastors who tell us they just don't have time to train competent people find the results of such a response obvious.

Where to Begin?

Assuming that your church or Christian organization does not have the advantage of starting fresh, how do you go about improving or inaugurating an effective volunteer program?

Start with Goals and Expectations

First, decide what it is you believe that needs to be done. We will say more later about bringing the people involved into the planning early in the process, but unless you clearly define your goals, there is no point in asking other people to have a part in them. (See chapter 1.) Outline your *expectations and assumptions* so that you know what you are requesting. How many hours of work will it require? What kind of standards of accountability are you looking for? Where will the task need to be accomplished? What kind of leadership will it need? If the paid staff needs a clear-cut job description, how much more does the volunteer! (And how seldom it is given to him.)

Have a People Policy

Second, expectations and job descriptions should be written on the basis of policies which *serve the best interest of the people involved*, not necessarily the organization (church). The church faces the continual dilemma of meeting the needs of its people and at the same time using them to serve the world. This is why the local church requires some of the most sophisticated leadership of any organization in the world. But if we are to have a biblical view of individuals, it follows that we must think about how these volunteers can grow in the experience and look back upon it as a building into their life.

If we can involve people around a common cause and at the same time meet their needs and develop their gifts and personalities, we will service both the means and the end of human relations.

People must be placed above administrative convenience in policies and procedures. It is a failure at this point which leads to failure of many volunteer programs. It must never be assumed that because a person has volunteered for a job, that from there on out he will be able to put up with all manner of inconvenience.

Look for Commonly Shared Goals

In recruiting volunteers from a group such as a local church, the best place to begin is with *their* goals. Search for people who are already interested and *therefore motivated* for the type of program that you want to promote. Bring in people at the planning stage. For example, by involving a large number of people in a planning conference you will often discover those who have a high interest in a particular kind of program.

Be very clear about responsibilities involved. If you err in any direction err on making the task seem more difficult than you really believe it is. People who are talked into something on the assumption that it will not take very much of their time, usually know in their heart that it is going to take a lot more than you have told them. They really don't perform very well. So, spell out the time limits of the job and any varying roles that they may have in it. If it is a job for one hour and that's it, say so. If it involves a higher commitment with some other somewhat hidden responsibilities, make sure they know these.

Training Is the Key

Training is the major key to using volunteers. Once a good training program is established, subsequent training becomes easier and easier. Obviously, if you are trying to build a group of volunteers in an organization which now has none, one of the first groups to recruit and train are the trainers! An open and frank discussion with the volunteer leadership of your organization will do much in this area. What kind of training do they believe is needed for their jobs? Where in the past have they felt that they didn't know enough to do the job adequately?

One excellent way to provide trainers is to have *three people for each job:* someone in training, someone carrying out the job, and someone who has done the job and is now acting as a coach. In this way you can show genuine continuity and give people the feeling that they are moving ahead. As an example, a man or woman might be asked to serve as a Sunday school superintendent for a three-year period, the first year of which would be as an assistant, the second year would be as superintendent, and the third year would be as a coaching assistant.

It is an excellent idea to appoint or elect volunteer leaders well in advance and to spell out these three possible phases of their task.

In any event, don't take training for granted. Make sure that the leadership of volunteer committees and volunteer task forces clearly spells out how the newcomers are going to be trained and how the group is going to *know* that they have been trained.

Putting Volunteers to Work

As you put volunteers to work give careful consideration to the interpersonal situation in which they are working. There is a vast difference between serving every day as a part-time volunteer in an office and serving on a board which meets once a month. In the first case the volunteer will usually have the warm support of the other people in the office, and will soon get to know them intimately. He will find his friendships here, and can look forward to knowing and being known. He will see himself fitting into a going organization, and will usually be pleased to be part of something where he can see output.

However, the volunteer serving on a board or a committee that meets only occasionally will need much more attention paid to needs of interpersonal relationships. As we suggest in chapter 31 on committees, time spent sharing and praying in groups of threes before a monthly meeting with subsequent reports back to that same group before moving into another at the following meeting will quickly build relationships among the group which transcend the work of the group.

Make it part of your announced goal for the volunteer program that people keep all relationships not only cordial but actively loving.

Establish Clear Delegation

Make sure that volunteers who have been given assignments know the level of delegation which has been given to them (see chapter 17) and that they know when they are to report back. This means that the paid leadership or the volunteer leadership must build into their own schedules a time to be actively listening and learning from the volunteer's experience.

Maintain Self-Esteem

Recognize the necessity of the volunteer to retain and to build his self-esteem. How often do we take a person highly qualified in one area and put him to work in another where he is not qualified (a bank president ushering on Sunday morning). Try to match the task to the skills of the individual and also make sure that it is meeting his need for learning.

Volunteers cannot be driven but they can and should be led. Just as a string cannot be pushed but can be pulled, so people are willing to follow if they feel that the leadership knows where it is going and if they are really part of an ongoing program.

Leadership needs to be generally concerned and care how volunteers feel. We must read feedback from them and let them know that we are hearing them. This means that we must never take volunteer work for granted. We need to be generous in praise and appreciation.

The Best Way

To recruit, train, and maintain the best volunteers, apply to a volunteer program the basic principles of good participative management you would use in a nonvolunteer organization.

Where to Use Volunteers

Where might there be some unexpected places to use volunteers? Analyze your own task and break it down into its many parts. Do the same for those people who are working for you, for instance, your secretary. Are there particular time sequences in which repetitive work is done at the same time of the day? Are there some specialty things for which you could call upon volunteers? Perhaps you need to build up a team of specialists in different areas such as law, insurance, building. Look for positions to train more volunteers. In any ongoing organization, theoretically, every volunteer should have a substitute whom he knows, is training, and upon whom he can call if he gets in a time bind himself.

23.

Need a New Secretary?

There are few things more important to the effective, successful executive than a good secretary. Whether you are the head of your denomination or a young pastor with only part-time help, your secretary can help you perform at your best or make you look your worst. Usage and time have a way of destroying the usefulness of words; "secretary" has not fared well. One person's secretary may be someone who can type, file, and answer the phone. Another may be truly an *executive* assistant, bringing order out of the chaos of the daily details and handling a myriad of responsibilities. Perhaps it is ignorance. Regardless of the reason, the Christian leader who has the privilege of having a secretary and is not using her to full advantage, is missing a real opportunity for personal growth and improved leadership.

We have already referred to a secretary as "her." This is not only a recognition of the current situation but also reflects a belief that, at least in our Western culture, women have some basic qualities that seem to fit hand-in-glove with the need of a manager or leader for an *executive* secretary. And just as we are limiting our discussion to "her," we will also speak mostly about the personal, executive secretary.

Basic Qualities

The particular way in which an executive and his secretary work together will and should be dependent on the executive's style, the way he goes about his job. But there are some basic qualities that we believe every executive should look for in a secretary.

Loyalty. Without it, you are defeated before you begin. It starts of course with the common and highest loyalty to God, for our Christian service is given to him. But there needs to be a complete loyalty to you. This need not come at the expense of loyalty to others or to the organization. But in it is implied a confidential relationship and trust. Your secretary sees you as you are.

Memory. Not very many secretarial books talk about it, but a good memory and especially what we would call a "connective memory," can do worlds to help your performance. The best of filing systems will fail. Calendars will be overlooked. Your desk may become a shambles. The secretary who can find "it" soon becomes invaluable (sometimes *too* invaluable).

Maturity. It *takes* maturity to maintain a pleasant smile in the face of an irate visitor, to know that the best of bosses will have a grouchy day, and to carry a warm, friendly, cheerful spirit, without being effusive or aggressive.

Insight. She needs to be able to learn how you think, to study your work habits, to become almost an alter ego. Her greatest value as an executive secretary is to be able to make decisions the way you would make them yourself.

Self-organization. Let's face it. Most executives are so busy organizing other people and things that we need someone to organize us. To do that, a secretary needs to be organized herself. This means planning her day in a way that permits interruptions. It means not being thrown by completely unexpected events. It means knowing where everything is and how to use the tools available.

Details. You may need to have the "big picture" continually before you. You may have a day filled with far-reaching decisions. But someone better pay attention to the details and that someone is usually your secretary. This is one of those cases where your example perhaps best be forgotten, for details are the little foxes that nibble at the vines. A good secretary will notice the details and see that they are handled or gently remind you that you had better handle them before they become big problems.

Model and Trainer. Just because she is an executive's secretary, many secretaries have the opportunity to train other staff, both by what they do and what they say.

Attractive. Not just physical attractiveness in clothes and grooming, but an attractiveness of attitude and spirit.

Skills. Certainly. But not just typing and shorthand skills. She needs interpersonal skills in handling people, an understanding of basic office procedures from simple accounting to how to get her typewriter repaired, not to mention travel planning and schedule juggling.

How to Find Such an Angel

Now if your secretary has all of these qualities already, blessed are you among executives. Suppose she doesn't? What can you do about it?

Perhaps you have to start with getting another one. How to hire and fire personnel in a Christian organization is the subject of another chapter. But maybe now is the time to face up to the fact that neither you nor your secretary is going to become what you should be in your present situation and start laying plans for a replacement.

Take your time in hiring a secretary. Look for a balance between enthusiasm, experience, and education. Check references by phone if you can. Look for a fit in your personalities and outlook. You are going to spend hundreds of hours with this person! Pay the extra expense of temporary help while waiting to get the right person.

How to Keep Her When You Find Her

Take time to train her. Put training times down on your calendar. A good secretary will eventually figure out what you are up to, but she will be twice as good if you help her. Expose her to all the people she will need to know. Personally introduce her to your peers and superiors. Lead her through any organizational procedures that may exist. Tell her your idiosyncrasies, likes and dislikes. Take time to tell her *why* as well as what.

Maintain communications. Set aside a few minutes at the beginning of the day to review with her your workload and hers. Let her help you figure out how you are going to get your job done and help her with hers.

Delegate clearly. There are many levels of delegation. Make sure she knows what decisions you want her to make and which are to come back to you. Do you want her to compose replies to letters before showing them to you? Which ones? What kind? Do you want her to maintain control over appointments, visitors and phone calls? Under what circumstances? How?

This is a very delicate area. Your secretary is "you" to many people. It is very difficult for them to question whether she is "interpreting" what you are saying, or actually giving a straight story. Encourage your secretary to develop mutual trust so that people feel free to come to her, and yet at the same time do not expect that they are going to get special favors.

Plan together. Your job is her job. The more she understands what you are up to, the more responsibility she can assume. Planning can take many forms. One of the best ways is to make sure that you have a calendar which reflects what you are doing. There's nothing more embarrassing for a secretary than not to know what her boss's plans are. This may involve a lot of calendar juggling, but in the long run it will pay off.

Let her initiate. Let her sort out the mail into things like "immediate attention," "look at today," and "reading." Have her read your mail and note things to be handled, replies needed, items someone else can handle. Assume she will dream up Plan B when Plan A fails, and teach her how to do it.

Give her ongoing training opportunities. Encourage her to attend training seminars, to join secretaries' societies, to take college level extension courses.

Pay her for the level at which she is working. If she is doing the job of an *executive* secretary, make certain that within the confines of your organization's salary structure she is paid as an executive secretary. (She may be worth more than some executives!)

Set high standards. Excellence is hard to attain, but it is worth the effort. If there is time to do a job over, there was probably time to do it right in the first place.

Increase her responsibility. Keep expanding her role as far and as fast as she can go. Plan on making her the best secretary you have known.

Appreciate her. It's so easy to get caught up in the day-by-day office routine that we fail to notice growth and improved performance or even the little jobs well done. How easy it is to be appreciative of everyone else and fail to give a well-deserved compliment to the one work-ing closest with us.

Maintain a professional relationship. The more effec-tively your secretary does her job, the more personal will become your relationship. This is an advantage. It is also your greatest point of vulnerability. How many men do you personally know who have destroyed their careers as the result of an improper liaison with their secretary? The reasons are obvious. Daily contact, a deep under-standing of your needs, a constant attention to your desires, all contribute to building a very attractive relation-ship. If this is combined with less than adequate support at home, the results can be disastrous. There's no easy an-swer to this one except to recognize the potential for trouble and to insist that you both act accordingly. Avoid situations that could be in any way compromising. It may cause inconvenience, but it will be worth it in the end.

Plan for her replacement. Early in the game have her start compiling a notebook on how you want things and how she does them. Most secretaries put off this kind of work since (at the moment) they have no intention of leav-ing. But to have a well-tabbed notebook on such things as letter format, handling phone calls, logging and filing letters, arranging trips, and handling expense sheets is worth many, many hours of frustration.

Additional Reading

Alec Mackenzie's excellent book, *The Time Trap*, de-votes an entire chapter to how to use your secretary effectively. It is an excellent chapter to review with your secretary as you seek to help her performance (Amacom, New York, 1972).

As basic handbooks, our secretaries both recommend

The Successful Secretary's Handbook by Esther Becker and Evelyn Anders (Harper & Row, 1971), and *Professional Secretary's Handbook* by Dr. Fred S. Cook and Lenore S. Forti (Dartnell Publications, 1971).

24.

Consultants

There comes a time in the life of every organization when the leadership feels like yelling, "Help!" It may be that the organization has become stagnant. Perhaps it is facing a problem which it has never encountered. It could even be it has been too successful, and its leadership is unable to manage in an enlarged world. For another organization it may be a matter of internal conflict, lack of agreement on where they should go next or how they should accomplish their objectives.

It is with this kind of environment that someone is likely to say, "Let's call in a consultant." Too often such a suggestion meets with the immediate approval of the rest of the leadership team. Here, they feel, may be the answer to all of their problems. "Let's bring in someone who really *knows*. Let's get an *unbiased* opinion. Let's find someone who can have a *fresh look*." And probably in a number of heads is the thought, "Besides if it doesn't work no one here will get blamed."

When Should You Use a Consultant?

Probably the best general answer is when you believe that you do not have the adequate resources within the organization to carry out the program or solve the problem that you face, whether the problem is organization-wide or in a very specific area, such as the need to set up a new accounting system.

Some General Guidelines

You may need a consultant when:

- more expert opinion in a specialized area is required.

- you have a problem or requirement which would require hiring considerable new staff.

- you are considering a reorganization.

- you are moving into a brand-new area of ministry.

- you have a short-term need for management assistance.

What Is a Consultant?

There are a wide range of individuals who are potentially available to help a local church or other Christian organization. They range from people whom we might call *facilitators* or *enablers* to specialists such as an outside accounting firm. They are generally people who have a demonstrated expertise in solving or handling certain kinds of problems or who work with firms that have specialized in certain areas. They may act as trainers, advisors, researchers, reflectors, or even as part of the regular management team.

What Will He Do?

Ask questions. Discover where you've been and where you are in a particular or general area. The point, of course, is that this will lead to recommendations on where you should go and what is the most expeditious way of getting there.

Where Do You Find Him?

It's not easy. Although there are many consulting firms, and you can find them listed under various headings in the Yellow Pages, there aren't very many people who have established a track record working as independent consultants, especially with Christian organizations. Probably the safest way to locate a consultant is to survey organizations or churches similar to your own to discover where they have used consultants, which ones they have used and what successes they have had. Certainly you should hesitate before engaging anyone who does not come recommended from organizations similar to yours. (This makes things rather tough on the new consultant, but makes it much safer for you.)

If you are related to a denomination, start there. Even if you are not, many denominations make their specialists available to others. Don't be afraid of the secular consulting firm, especially if your need is in a specialty area such as accounting, salary administration, or office procedures. Just make sure *you* define your need.

Sometimes you can get quite a bit of "free" consultation from equipment suppliers. For example, manufacturers of special office furniture will often do a work-flow analysis for you as part of their equipment proposal.

How Do You Go About Engaging One?

The first step is to do your very best to define exactly the need that you believe a consultant will meet. Try to get this down in writing, preferably on one page. Make sure that all the people who are involved have a shared belief that this is a true picture of the situation. It may be that your problem is so nebulous that you'll be unable to define it as clearly as you would like. It is not uncommon to do some preliminary reflecting with a management consultant to nail down your problem.

After you have defined specifically what you want done, start compiling a list of possible candidates to do your particular job. Do your search through churches, seminaries, other Christian organizations and get as many references as you can. Use the telephone. It's quicker and more effective. Remember the better consultants are going to have a backlog of work and you may be forced to fit your need into someone else's schedule.

After you have made an initial contact, if at all possible, have a face-to-face meeting with the consultant to explain your problem to him. Ask him to respond back to you in writing with his understanding of your need and his recommendations as to how to proceed.

From this you can essentially write a letter to him requesting a proposal. Be as specific as you can. Many times you will need a proposal to do a preliminary study on which a future proposal can be made. Do your best to try to define the problem in such clear terms that it will be possible for you to engage a different type of consultant if the initial study shows that this is what you need.

Have a contract and a clear understanding of what is expected in terms of reports, output, or any other type of documentation for which you are asking.

How Do You Prepare for Him?

Make certain that all the people involved are alerted ahead of time. There is nothing more disconcerting than to be called in and be introduced as Mr. Smith "who is going to look into some problems for us." This doesn't mean that you have to announce to everyone in the organization that you're engaging a consultant. It does mean that people have to have an understanding of why he is there and what is expected of *them*. Otherwise a consultant can be very threatening and will receive little cooperation on the part of the people with whom he may have to work.

Do your very best to gather all the necessary documentation together. Remember you are going to pay for a consultant's time, and anything you can do to save that time will be to your advantage.

"Free up" people to be with him. Again, the consultant is going to cost you considerably more than the time of the people with whom he is going to be dealing.

What Will It Cost?

Quite a bit. Remember that the average consultant is working for himself. The actual number of hours he will be with a customer may be small as compared to the number of hours that he will have to spend traveling and preparing or analyzing what has been done. If he is working on a per diem or an hourly basis you may find yourself paying as much as $300 to $400 a day for his services. This is where you need to be definitive in terms of what he is going to do. You are much better off to write a definitive contract in which you engage the consultant to do a specified study over a given period of time and to produce a specific kind of report after having spent a given number of hours with you and your staff.

The Management Consultant

This person usually has a considerable number of years in the management level of different kinds of organizations. Typically, he can be used to analyze the organizational structure with an eye toward clarifying purposes and goals and thus recommend changes in the organization that will make it more effective. He can also help write job descriptions for executive positions. He is a generalist but usually conversant with a number of different management specialty areas, such as computers, accounting, office procedures, and so forth.

The Computer System Consultant

This person should typically have had experience in managing a computer system for an organization similar or considerably more complex than yours. He should be able to give you counsel on whether the use of electronic data processing will enhance your organization and whether you should consider installing your system in-house or go into a computer service bureau. He may be used to help design the total system for you, or to oversee the design of a system by people other than those in your own organization.

The Enabler or Facilitator

This is a term that is used for a number of people who work specifically in churches and other volunteer organizations. These are people who typically have experience in the behavioral sciences, particularly in communication. Many times they act as trainers in helping committees and others learn how to function better.

The Church Consultant

The local church is an extremely complex organization. It requires a very special understanding. As a result, there are very few experienced church consultants. The best ones are those who are sensitive to the fact that any time a church is going through a time of major transition, it does well to do a self-analysis. Such times include the call of a new pastor, a noticeable increase or decrease in attendance and/or membership, the contemplation of or *the* end of a building program.

The Fund-Raising Consultant

Don't confuse this person with the fund *raiser*. There are many individuals and organizations in the business of doing fund raising for you. The consultant to the local church can give counsel on the "how to" as well as answer the question "how much?" Many consultants will lay out a program for you, but will expect you to do the work.

The Public Relations Consultant

This title covers a wide range of activities from seeing that your organization gets good press coverage to giving counsel in fund raising. Many work on a continuing retainer basis.

The Specialist

There are a surprisingly large number of persons who offer their services as consultants in specialty areas. These include accounting, training, personnel management, salary structures, office procedures, building services, transportation, direct mail, and almost any other area that you can think of. If it is a well-established procedure or function or area of service, there is probably someone who is acting as a consultant in the field.

What Are the Advantages?

The major advantage is that you get the benefit of other organizations' successes and failures, hopefully wrapped up in the person of the consultant. At the same time you get relatively unbiased opinions of your situation. This is particularly true when you call in a consultant to survey your effectiveness with a definite understanding that there will be no possibility of his becoming involved in any solution which he may recommend. Another advantage is lower overall costs. When one takes into account the cost of hiring, maintaining and training an individual in a special area, the consultant's apparent high cost may turn out to be the least expensive way to go.

A Few Consultants

Christian Resource Associates, P.O. Box 2100, Orange, California 92669.

Yokefellow Institute, 920 Earlham Drive, Richmond, Indiana 47374, is especially skilled at church consultation.

Denominational headquarters.

Church Consultation Service, 177 N. Madison Avenue, Pasadena, California 91101.

PART FOUR

Managing Your Time

25.

Managing Your Time

An executive basically has five things with which he works.

1. *Manpower.* A leader always works with people.

2. *Resources.* This would include money, equipment, property, etc.

3. *Information.* In today's cybernetic society, information becomes increasingly valuable as a factor with which an executive works and a tool which he uses in his leadership.

4. *Experience.* Experience allows the executive to make proper and valid judgments.

5. *Time.* Christians particularly should be concerned about time for the Bible has so much to say about it.

Time is the raw material of life. The passing of each day brings to us the opportunity to evolve into something better than we were at the start of the day. As the Apostle Peter encourages us to "grow in the grace and knowledge of our Lord and Savior Jesus Christ" (2 Pet. 3:18), this takes place within a time span. Our personal success, or lack of it, is largely contingent upon the effective use of our time.

We All Have the Same Amount

Time is immensely valuable and utterly irretrievable. Without doubt it is the most valuable commodity we have. No one has more—or less—time than you and I. To each of us is given the 1440 minutes per day and the 168 hours per week. We all have the same amount of time in every day as does everyone else. This is true whether it be the paperboy or the president, the author or the homemaker, the farmer or the preacher. The clocks we buy run at the same rate. Even our Lord Jesus Christ had exactly the same amount of hours in his day, but think of the *quality* of his time investment.

We All Waste Time

Yet, in spite of its preciousness and vast potentialities, there is nothing we squander quite so thoughtlessly as time.

As the wise and pragmatic Sir Walter Scott has said, "Dost thou love life? then do not squander time, for that's the stuff life is made of."

Time is a many-faceted . . . paradoxical . . . an ever-changing/never-changing phenomenon. It has no substitute, it waits for no man, and it takes its toll on all men.

For all of us time is in short supply and high demand. There never seems to be enough of it.

There is an urgency attached to time. Our Lord Jesus Christ felt it when he said, "I must work the works of him that sent me, while it is day: the night cometh, when no man can work" (John 9:4, KJV). The pioneer missionary Robert Moffatt felt it when he said, "We shall have all eternity in which to celebrate our victories, but we have only one short hour before the sunset in which to win them."

Our supply of time is totally perishable. The only variable available to us is the *use* that we make of our finite supply of time. It is important that we budget the time we have to spend just as carefully as we budget the money we have to spend.

Time's business calls for a budget. There is a time to pray and a time to play; the time-thrifty Christian neglects neither, uses both.

Time can be our tool; we need not be its slave.

Time Management Is Self-Management

Peter Drucker has written, "Time management takes perseverance and self-discipline, but no other investment pays higher dividends."

Time is not saved by multiplying devices. It is saved by manly discipline. It is the man, not the mechanics, that will make the difference.

Time is but a measurement—a dimension. Thus it, per se, can scarcely be our problem. When we look into the matter of time and its management all roads ultimately lead back to the management of ourselves. The entire science of management deals with the way executives allocate their time.

We so often hear, "I wish I knew how to manage my time better." Rarely do we hear, "I wish I knew how to manage myself better." For better time utilization we must learn to manage ourselves.

A great deal is said and preached regarding the stewardship of wealth and possessions; less is said about the stewardship of talent; little is said concerning the stewardship of time. Possibly it is even less understood. As Christians we will be held accountable for our use of the time given to us. In Colossians 4:5 the Apostle Paul says, "Make the best possible use of your time" (Phillips). Again, in Ephesians 5 Paul says, "Look carefully then how you walk, not as unwise men but as wise, making the most of the time, because the days are evil" (v. 15).

211

Our mental attitude in the use of time is most important. If we don't want to do something, we can find a thousand reasons for not doing it. It may be too far or too hot or too cold or too wet or too dry. But, if we want to do something nothing will stop us—obstacles are brushed aside as if they were nothing.

We all ask the question, "Where has the time gone?" This rhetorical question certainly misstates the case. Time doesn't depart the scene; it simply passes at the rate it always has, while we accomplish far less than perhaps we should have. Better to ask, "How could I have planned so poorly and left so much to be done in so little time?"

Time Management Questions

When a newspaper reporter writes his story he consciously or unconsciously answers one of a half dozen questions in his lead sentence—*who, what, when, why, where,* and *how.* In planning activities—all of which involve time —we might ask ourselves the same kind of questions.

In answering *who*—we may delegate—find someone else who is available.

In answering *what* we may simplify.

In answering *when* we may postpone or set up.

In answering *why* we may eliminate the job altogether.

In answering *where* we may combine the place of sequence.

In answering *how* we may improve or make shortcuts.

Start with Time Management

It is generally conceded that a salesman's success is nine-tenths management of time and one-tenth territory. Quoting Peter Drucker again, he says that, "Those executives who really get things done don't start with their work, they start with their time." In other words they carve out the time necessary for initiating and becoming creative rather than simply reacting to the pressures of the moment, whether it be correspondence, the telephone, conferences, etc.

It has been suggested that there are three magic questions of time management. These are:

1. What am I now doing that does not need to be done by me or anyone else? This includes the process of elimination.

2. What am I now doing that should be done by someone else? This involves delegation.

3. What am I now doing that wastes my time or other people's time?

Where to Begin

Where does one begin in managing his time? How do we get more things done? If you think about it a moment the answer is obvious:

1. Decide what it is that you want to do with your life. Set *goals*.

2. Establish *priorities* for the goals that you set.

3. Figure out how to reach these goals. This is *planning*.

4. Follow a procedure which will use the least amount of time to reach them. *Schedule*.

What then are needed are goals, priorities, and plans.

Priority Selection Is Key

The leader must be meticulously careful in the selection of his priorities. If it be ambition to excel that marks us, there must be selection and rejection, then concentration on the things of paramount importance. Striving for excellence in one's work, whatever it may be, is not only a Christian's duty but a basic form of Christian witness. This could be called a foundation of nonverbal communication which supports the verbal.

The few people who seem to do an incredible number of things do them one thing at a time, according to a priority schedule they have set up. This means they also can do it much faster than those who try so many things at once. In other words they concentrate, they set priorities and stick to them.

Remember—it is not how much *we do* that counts, but how much we *get done!*

Posteriorities Are Important Too!

Setting priorities really is not too difficult. The harder task is setting posteriorities. That is, what tasks not to tackle—and sticking to the decision. Have you noted that what one postpones one oftentimes abandons?

There's Always Enough Time

Remember, there are enough hours in each day for us to fulfill God's perfect and particular plan for our lives. We never need more time than we have to do the whole will of God. This truth is so liberating. As the late Adlai Stevenson said, "It's not the days of your life but the life in your days that counts."

Take Time

Take time to work—it is the price of success.
Take time to think—it is the source of power.
Take time to play—it is the secret of perpetual youth.
Take time to read—it is the fountain of wisdom.
Take time to be friendly—it is the road to happiness.
Take time to dream—it is hitching your wagon to a star.

Take time to love and be loved—it is the privilege of redeemed people.
Take time to look around—it is too short a day to be selfish.
Take time to laugh—it is the music of the soul.
Take time for God—it is life's only lasting investment.

Additional Reading

Managing Your Time by Ted Engstrom and Alec Mackenzie ties time management into organization management. Available in paperback from Zondervan.

Tools for Time Management by Ed Dayton will give you a host of particular time-management concepts (Zondervan, 1974).

James T. McCay takes a more introspective approach in his *The Management of Time* (Prentice-Hall, 1959).

If you really want to blow your mind on the whole *idea* of time, dip into *The Future of Time*, edited by Henri Yaker, Humphrey Osmond, and Frances Cheek (Anchor, 1972).

26.

What Next?
Establishing Priorities

How surprising it is that many people who never knowingly throw away their life are willing to let their life slip through their hands in little pieces just because they haven't decided what are the important things in life. Consequently they are at a constant loss as to what to do next. Often we hear someone say, "That's not one of my priorities. I can't do that today." Sometimes this statement reflects a well-balanced approach to priorities. Too often it may mean nothing more than "as far as I can tell right now, that's not what I want to do."

How Do You Set Priorities?

Almost any Christian executive if pressed could tell you what the steps are to setting up priorities.

1. Decide what it is that you really want to do with your life. Are your goals recognizable? Do you really know what you want to have happen?

2. Establish priorities for the goals that you have set.

3. Work out a system whereby these goals will be reached and measured.

4. Follow a procedure which will use the least amount of time and resources to reach these goals.

But as simple as that procedure seems, most of us have a great deal of difficulty following it. Why is this so?

Obstacles to Good Priorities

Probably the greatest difficulty that most of us have in setting goals and establishing priorities is that we do not have an understanding that we must deal with *the whole man*. If we as Christians believe that all of our actions and opportunities are somehow related to the grand purposes of God, then *all of our life* must reflect a consistent view that personal goals—what we should do and what we should be—need to be considered side-by-side with the "work" that God has given us to do.

A second, often missed ingredient to good priorities is the need for a Christian value system. Most of us immediately respond to such a statement, "Well, of course I have a Christian value system!" But a value system is useless unless it has been worked out within the culture and humdrum of everyday life which face us. Each one of us must decide what is important *today* in this situation.

The Christian leader must be especially careful in his selection of priorities. If it be for each of us a sanctified ambition to excel and to honor Christ, there must be selection and rejection, and then concentration on the things of paramount importance. We can't do everything. Lesser things must be left off so we can do greater things.

A Christian Value System

A Christian value system is obviously one which is biblically based. How each one of us will work out our own life-style will be dependent upon our personal gifts, our commitments, our calling, and the situation in which God has placed us. But there *are* some ultimates, and there are some basic underlying priorities that all of us should consider.

As Christians, we know that our ultimate goal is to give glory to God and to enjoy him forever. But in the many opportunities we have to give glory to God, there are certain levels of priorities, certain levels of commitment upon which everything else hangs.

Our first commitment is to God through Christ. Most of us are sure that we have made this commitment, but it is one that needs to be reasserted on a daily basis; for which we need to explore new ways of working it out week-by-week.

Our second commitment is to the body of Christ. Jesus thought that this was so important that he called it a *new* commandment: "A new commandment I give you, that you love one another; even as I have loved you, that you also love one another. By this all men will know that you are my disciples, if you have love for one another" (John 13:34, 35).

I John 3:23 tells us that the measure of our Christian performance is our love for one another. Christ, in his prayer in John 17, indicates that the way the world will believe that he has been sent from the Father is that his disciples are one, even as he and the Father are one (John 17:21).

A third commitment is to the work of Christ, the task that God has given us to do.

It is surprising how often we move directly from the first commitment to the third and completely leave out the second. And yet the New Testament epistles have much, much more to say about the loving relationships within the body of Christ than they do about the work of Christ. The New Testament assumes that when this love exists, the witness and work will go forth. In fact the often quoted statement of Christ to his disciples in Acts 1:8 does not say that you *should be* my witnesses, nor does it say, *you can be* my witnesses, rather it says "you *shall be* my witnesses, in Jerusalem, and in all Judea, and in Samaria, and to the end of the earth.''

We miss this point in setting our priorities to our personal peril.

Working Out Christian Priorities

If these three basic levels of priorities are correct, then how might they work out in our priority planning? Assume that you have a whole list of goals, things that you wanted to *do*, things that you wanted to *be*; based on these three levels of priorities, how might you work them out?

Since the best way to maintain your priorities is to fill up your calendar with all of the events that reflect your personal goals in life, if your calendar reflects correct priorities, then you will have a tremendous defense against all of the things that tend to distract you from what you want to do and be. So, imagine for a moment that you are sitting down, planning a calendar for the coming months and you are going to fill in the calendar based upon the priorities we have given so far. Where would you begin? We believe your calendar should be filled up in this order:

1. *Time with God.* That time when you are going to seek him in worship, prayer, his word, that top priority time which must be there. (Remember it is not the amount of time, but the *quality* of your time that counts!)

2. *Time with the family.* If our second general priority is that of being with the body of Christ, then certainly the most important part of that body is your family. When is there going to be time when you build yourself into their lives and let them build themselves into yours? This ought to reflect special times with your wife, dates with your children, time to play, time to talk, time which is considered just as important (and many times more important!) than any other time.

3. *Time with the family of God.* This would include worshiping, praying, fellowship. It would be both with the larger body of believers and with small groups.

4. *Time for yourself.* When are you going to have some relief from the pressures? Do you have time for golf? Or bowling? Or to do some relaxed reading? There ought to be times put aside *on your calendar*, in which you may not even know until that moment what you will do with them, but which reflect the fact that there are basic needs which you have as an individual, needs which must be met if you are going to be an effective Christian leader.

5. *Time for other people.* This is over and above your regular work commitments. It recognizes that you are related to other people and you are going to have to have time for *their goals*. This means blocks of time on your calendar which might say nothing on them but "others."

6. *Time to plan.* This is one of the most overlooked schedule items. It is important not only to review progress against goals, but in making new plans for future performance. This probably ought to be reviewed a bit longer for each week and even at greater length each month.

7. *Time for the tasks to which God has called you.* That which we normally call "work." (What an inappropriate term!)

Priority Considerations

There are certain questions which ought to be asked in the matter of setting priorities. For example:

1. How urgent is it? Should it be done right now? Today? Soon? Some day?

2. How important is it? Very? Quite? Somewhat? Not so much?

3. How often must it be done? Daily? Weekly? Sometimes?

4. Can someone else do it more effectively than I? No? Perhaps? Yes? (If yes, delegate it.)

5. Is it part of a larger task or goal that I am committed to?

6. Is this the best way?

Remember the words of the late General Eisenhower, "Urgent matters are seldom important, important matters are seldom urgent!"

One way of using these questions is to set up a priority check list in which you list the goal on the left hand side and then list the above questions across the top. Take an 8½-by-11-inch piece of paper and lay it on its side and put headlines across the top which might be Goals, Importance, Frequency, Delegation, Larger Goal, Impact, Best Way.

How to Establish Priorities

Assuming that you have listed your goals toward God, toward the family of God, and toward the work of God, how can you go about establishing priorities? Here are some:

1. List all of your goals. Get them out where you can see them and begin to evaluate them.

2. Make sure each of these goals is measurable.

3. Analyze the "why" of each. Eliminate those which have no Christian basis or which do not fit into your overall value system.

On the basis of your value system and this above analysis, you might want to divide this list into A, B, C's: A—those things which *must* be done, or are very important; B—those that should be done, or somewhat important; and C—those that *can* be done, not so important.

The good thing about this A, B, C system is that it helps

you to recognize that many times there is no *one* outstanding priority, there may be four or five "A's."

Maintaining Your Priorities

Setting goals and re-setting priorities is a continuing process. A continual review of your planning must include a continual review of your goals, therefore, a continual review of your priorities.

A few people who seem to do an incredible number of things, do them one at a time. They set up a priority schedule. This means they can also do the task much faster than those who try to do many things at once. In other words, they concentrate, they set priorities, and they stick to them.

After all, it's not how much we *do* that counts, but how much we get done.

27.

What's on Your Calendar?

We are living in a day in which the number of "interpersonal intersections" is rising at a rate faster than most of us can handle. The managing of our time becomes a major preoccupation for most Christian leaders. Most of us have discovered that we need some kind of appointment book or calendar upon which to keep track of commitments that we have made to others and to ourselves for our time. But as is true with all types of human endeavors, the more time we invest in planning, the less is the likelihood that we will be surprised or disappointed at the outcome. This means that for the busy Christian executive there is a constant need to understand and display to himself and others his time commitments (appointments).

In chapter 26 we discussed our personal view of Christian priorities. We spelled out that we believe that if one was able to start with a blank calendar, he should start making appointments that reflected a priority system of first, commitment to God, second, commitment to his Body (with emphasis on self and family), and third, commitment to Christ's work (task commitments). Having such a priority system permits one to do some long-range evaluation as to the type of personal commitment he is making.

But since the magnitude of the commitment can only be measured in time, some kind of calendar is needed to reflect individual or group commitments.

The amount of detailed description that we need concerning our appointments or commitments is directly related to their immediacy—how soon we have to meet the commitment. We need a detailed list of what we are going to do today, or perhaps for the rest of the week. We need a less detailed, but overall view of what we are going to do for the coming month. We probably need only a broad view of what we are going to do for the coming year, and just a rough idea of the *specifics* of the years after that. For this kind of planning we may need one or more of three types of calendars, or appointment systems: Daily, monthly, and yearly. Some of us will also need a multiple-year schedule.

What's Available

Fortunately all of these systems are currently available. Most of them have their drawbacks. Most of them take *time* to use. How much time we should invest in using them should depend upon how much more effective they can help us become. We'll explore this further below.

One of the major difficulties with most of the calendar systems that are available is that they are based on a twelve-month year which (as the Chinese are fond of pointing out) is rather an old-fashioned, agricultural concept that the Western world still hangs onto. Consequently it is very difficult to buy a 1977 calendar until late in 1976, which means that if we purchase next year's calendar about October we can have someplace to write appointments for the next fourteen months (November and December of the present year and the twelve months of the following year). But as we proceed through the months ahead our ability to

226

keep track of our future commitments becomes shorter and shorter until finally by September of the following year we are looking only three months ahead (unless we've gone out and drawn up our own calendar). Calendar companies probably know what they're doing. No doubt there just hasn't been the demand by individuals.* Most corporations solve this problem by designing their own calendars. In any event, yearly calendars are available in sizes from about 10-by-15-inches to 24-by-30-inches. The ones which we have found the most useful have the months running across the top with the days running vertically.

Manufacturers of the typical 8½-by-11-inch desk top monthly calendar do a little better. Many times they will add an extra three months so that you can overlap into the next year, which gives you about a six-month lead on the future. The same is true of some of the monthly pocket calendars that are available. Like the yearly calendar, this type of monthly calendar, which typically has a block about 1-by-1½-inches for each day, is fine for noting major events, but usually does not have enough room to put down a daily schedule.

There are a number of both pocket size and desk top daily calendars available. The pocket type that is the most useful is one that combines not only a place for appointments, but also a list of things to do and a place to keep a time record of things actually done. A number of these systems are now available with a separate booklet for each month. Systems like those sold by Day-Timer, Inc. (Allentown, Pennsylvania 18001) and Seven Star Diary (available at most stationery stores) also have a place to put in a monthly spread, as well as the daily notations.

---

*One exception we know of is the Pryor Marking Company's Plan-A-Date which does comes out a year in advance. Their address is 21 East Hubbard Street, Chicago, Illinois 60611.

Which Kind Is Best?

It could very well be that you need all three! A yearly calendar mounted on the wall is an excellent way of showing major events that are going to be coming in future months. These might be organizational events that are going to demand your personal involvement or of which you should take note. This is also an excellent place to indicate by some form of symbols (such as an X or colored dots) when you are going to be out of the office or out of town. By using different color code markers you can do the same for other members of your staff. Having such a calendar available means that you are able to continually visualize your total commitments for twelve months ahead. One way to get around the problem of maintaining a continuous twelve-month overview is to mount the *next* year's yearly wall calendar underneath the present year's calendar and then to cut off the strip for each month that passes. This will uncover the equivalent month of the next year. (Of course, if you can't get next year's calendar during January of the current year, you may have to construct your own which is easily done by "reassembling" [a euphemism for cut-and-paste] a current year's wall calendar.)

The monthly calendar is a good device in that it gives you a quick overview of the type of involvements you have for the month. Some people use this calendar just to note non-routine events such as breakfasts, lunches, evening meetings, or dates when they are going to be away from their office or on which they are having visitors with whom they want to meet. Of course one could put this same kind of information on a wall calendar, but the difficulty is usually that a wall calendar has to be placed in such a position that you can't conveniently get at it while you're on the telephone or working at your desk. (You may also not want to spell out all of your personal appointments for the public to see.)

The one-month daily appointment book, such as the Day-Timer, with a place for "Things to Do" has many advantages. In addition to being able to plan your day in considerable detail, you can also put down a "laundry list" of things that you want to do on that particular day. You can also note down things in advance. In other words, if you know that you're not going to be able to get to an item until a week from today, or you know that that's the day on which it *should* be done, you can write it down on your appointment book under the "Things to Be Done" section.

Make Your Own

Figure 9 is a copy of a "homemade" daily appointment calendar and "Things to Do" list that was designed by Bob Larson, on our World Vision staff in Hong Kong. After attending a management seminar we conducted in Hong Kong, Bob came up with this way of grouping different kinds of things on his daily calendar.

Fill Up the Calendar

The only way to manage time is to control it, and the only way to control it is to decide *ahead* of time what is going to be done (or not done) during that period. The use of the "standard day" is helpful here. Start filling up your calendar with times with God, times with your family, times with the rest of the body of Christ, times for your own personal relaxation and planning, and then leave blocks of unscheduled time for others, time in which you're going to try to meet their goals. Make *written down* dates with your children and your wife and with your friends, and keep these priorities high. By filling up the calendar in this manner you give yourself an excellent defense against becoming overloaded with things which do not meet your priorities. If someone asks you if you can do something on Friday night, and your calendar tells you that you have a date with your son that evening, you can respond, "I'm sorry, I have a commitment." Of course, there are some people who will ask you what that commitment is, and it is at this point that your *real* priorities will begin to show! If you have put a block of time down for "others," don't schedule your own meetings or your own work during that time, but let it fill up with needs that other people have. This will make you an available person and will give you a great deal of freedom to be able to meet with other people. Again you will need to fight hard to keep regular business from interfering with such "time for others."

Communicating with Calendars

Calendars are an excellent communication device, both in the family and in the organization.

If your wife is keeping some kind of an appointment book or calendar, a weekly comparison by the two of you of your month ahead and some routine questions about how you're investing your time and with whom you're spending it can be an excellent communication tool. When you're talking about something *objective* such as a calendar, it's a lot easier for your wife or husband to bring up such questions about how much time you're spending at the office.

The same type of analysis can be applied to the whole family. One of the ways of controlling the perennial problem of TV overload is to decide as a family how many hours the TV set is going to be on during a given week and then to put down on the calendar which programs are going to be on when. Pull the plug the rest of the time.

Your appointment book and calendar are an excellent way to communicate between you and your secretary. The first-thing-in-the-morning review with your secretary of your appointments for the day and the week that lies ahead will give her a much better understanding and grasp of what you're up to. Her calendar should duplicate yours. And by the way, don't forget to ask her what *her* schedule is. She has some workload problems too.

Publishing a copy of your monthly calendar or exchanging copies of monthly calendars between members of the staff is an excellent way to understand what the other person is about and also to find appropriate times when you can get together. One pastoral team we know of had a regular time of reviewing each other's monthly calendars and having an open discussion about how the staff was spending its time. In one company that we know of, each engineer was asked to keep a monthly calendar on the drawer-pull of his desk. In this way anyone would know where he would be at a given period of time.

Which Is Best for You?

That's something that only you can answer. Perhaps you need to think more about a standard day or to do a weekly time inventory, as is suggested by most management experts, to see how you're actually spending your time and how much need you have to control it.

DAILY PLANNING SHEET   Date _____

Letters to Write   Phone Calls to Make
— _____   — _____
— _____   Person   No.
— _____   — _____
— _____   — _____
— _____   — _____

People to see   — _____
— _____   — _____
— _____   — _____
— _____   — _____
— _____   Appointments
— _____

Things to be Done

— _____	6:00 _____
— _____	6:30 _____
— _____	7:00 _____
— _____	7:30 _____
— _____	8:00 _____
— _____	8:30 _____
— _____	9:00 _____
— _____	9:30 _____
— _____	10:00 _____
— _____	10:30 _____
— _____	11:00 _____
— _____	11:30 _____
— _____	12:00 _____
— _____	12:30 _____
— _____	1:00 _____
— _____	1:30 _____
— _____	2:00 _____
Things to be Planned	2:30 _____
— _____	3:00 _____
— _____	3:30 _____
— _____	4:00 _____
— _____	4:30 _____
— _____	5:00 _____
— _____	5:30 _____
— _____	6:00 _____
Items to be Obtained	6:30 _____
	7:00 _____
— _____	7:30 _____
— _____	8:00 _____
— _____	8:30 _____
— _____	9:00 _____
— _____	9:30 _____
▲ Write priority in this column	10:00 _____

Figure 9

28.

Meetings!

Nobody seems to have much good to say about them. Everybody goes to them. Many of us spend a good deal of our life in them. And yet there is probably very little understanding about the human dynamics of meetings.

Meetings can be classified in a number of different ways, all of which are useful to us as we try to make them more effective. In what follows, we are going to limit ourselves to the task-oriented meeting as opposed to the fellowship meeting. The first has to do with two or more people coming together to accomplish something outside of themselves. The latter, in our present definition, is limited to people coming together for mutual encouragement and building each other up.

Different Kinds of Meetings

Meetings are formal and informal which is probably another way of saying that some are planned ahead of time and many more are impromptu.

Meetings are special or on-going. By this we mean that some meetings are set up on a continuous basis. They are regular meetings of a committee or a group, and to a large degree, each meeting is a continuation of the one that precedes it, and a base upon which the next one is built. Special meetings are those called to handle special problems or tasks.

Another way of looking at meetings has to do with the experience that the participants have in working with one another. The group that is working together for forty hours a week in the same organization, rubbing shoulder-to-shoulder on a number of problems each day, can and will operate in a much more different mode when it comes to a meeting than will a group of people who are meeting each other for the first time. This is a particularly important consideration for volunteer organizations. We will say more about it in what follows.

In their book *Creative Management* (John Wiley and Sons, New York, 1962), Norman Maier and John Hayes point out that meetings also need to be described in terms of their purpose. They identified three basic kinds of meetings: first, to announce or inform; second, to obtain the support of the group, the decision already having been made as to the outcome; and three, the problem-solving meeting. Their interesting book gives some excellent examples of what happens when the individual thinks that he is in the last kind of meeting, and he is really in the first or second kind!

Meetings Have a Poor Image

Meetings form a very real part of our society, and yet they have a rather poor track record in the minds of most people. We are all familiar with the definition of a camel as being a horse that was designed by a committee. The fact that there are so many camels wandering about the wastelands of many Christian organizations bears testimony to the fact that we need to learn a great deal more about the dynamics of meetings. Meetings are interpersonal intersection points. They are particularly *human* events. Because of the limitation of space, we will deal with meetings from the viewpoint of the organizer and leader, but much needs to be said about how to be an effective participant in a meeting. Participants need to understand that they are playing a special role which demands a responsibility to the group. No matter how brief or how long the meeting may be during this time, de facto organization has been formed with its own set of rules of communication, power structures, goals, and needs. The effective meeting participant is the one who can quickly size up the situation, the communication that is taking place, the competence of the people to discuss the subject that is at hand, the direction in which the group seems to be moving, and what is needed to obtain the goals of the meeting.

Elements of Any Good Meeting

It is simple to spell out the elements of a good meeting. It is much harder to carry them out.

1. Know the *purpose* of the meeting. Where does it fit in the overall structure of the organization or the situation in which you are in?

2. Set *goals* for the meeting. What is it that is to be accomplished during this encounter? How will you know that it has happened?

3. Select the right *participants*. Who needs to contribute what?

4. Do your *homework* and insure that other participants have done theirs.

5. Select the right *location*. The environment in which a meeting is carried out says a great deal about the meeting.

6. Bring the adequate communication *tools* and resources to the meeting.

7. Prepare an *agenda* and inform everyone adequately

as to what is going to happen. Use the agenda as a motivational tool to keep the meeting moving toward the goal. Summarize results of previous meetings before beginning.

8. *Keep the meeting moving* towards the direction in which it is supposed to be headed or realistically announce to the participants that the goal of the meeting has changed.

9. Announce what has been *accomplished*, who is responsible to take the next steps and what are the unresolved questions.

10. Announce what *action* will be taken in the future to handle the open items and unresolved questions. Record and distribute action items after the meeting.

How specific and detailed you will be in using these major points for any meeting will of course depend upon the meeting. However, even for an impromptu or informal meeting it is a good idea to pull out a piece of paper and at least write down the goal and the apparent facts, and agree on these before you begin. It's also a good idea at this time to decide what time you're going to adjourn.

Participants Need to Know Each Other

When a group is being brought together for the first time, where they may not know each other very well, particularly in the volunteer organization, a great deal of attention needs to be put to the needs of the participants. The better the participants understand each other's needs and current personal situation, the more likely they are to take these into account, and therefore produce a better flow of communication. There are a number of ways of doing this. In the formal organization situation write the stated goal or purpose of the meeting or series of meetings that is to follow on an easel or blackboard. Underneath list the names of the individuals with a statement as to their expertise, background or why they have been invited to come to this meeting. Many times it is also useful to have each participant make some opening statement about himself or about the task that lies ahead.

Meetings of Volunteers

In a volunteer organization, such as a local church, where people may have been elected to a committee position, it is even more important that an exploration be made of individual needs and that time be set aside for the group to get to know each other. A number of churches have used the approach of breaking up a group of twelve or more people into groups of three, and asking the subgroups to share with each other some particular prayer need that they have at this time. After the sharing time, the group of three can pray about what the need is and commit itself to continue to pray until the next meeting. At the next meeting, the same group of three meets together again and shares what has happened as a result of that prayer and then immediately breaks up into a new group of three for a new time of sharing. Over a period of twelve months this cements a group together very effectively. Those who want to "get on with the business of the meeting" will be surprised how much smoother the meeting will go because of the mutual understanding that exists at a personal level.

Make the Purpose Clear

Based on Maier and Hayes' analysis, the real purpose of the meeting should be announced early in the meeting. If it is a meeting to obtain group support for an idea already decided by a higher level, this should be made clear. It is true that individuals do use meetings to manipulate a group to accomplish that for which they do not want to be responsible for by themselves. However, getting group support is in many cases a very legitimate operation. If adequate homework has been done, and the group trusts the performance and integrity of the leader, then there is no reason why it should not stand behind the decision that is being made and lend its official support to the decision.

Many meetings will contain elements of all three types: announcement, consensus, and problem-solving. It is important that when the character of the meeting is shifting from one to the other that the leader announce what is happening. This is where an agenda can be particularly effective.

Using an Agenda

The agenda can be used in a number of ways. It can state the purpose and goals of the meeting. It can spell out the items that will be covered, the time frame in which they are to be covered, and the individuals who are responsible. If the agenda is in front of everyone or on a blackboard or easel where it can be checked off as the meeting progresses, then it can be used as an effective tool by the chairman or any of the participants in keeping the group to the question at hand. Even in informal meetings it is a good idea to scratch out an agenda and to state clearly what the time frame is.

What about Minutes?

Minutes are probably the most abused and misused part of any meeting. How much the minutes need to recount all of the details of a meeting is generally dependent on the time between meetings on the same subject and whether such a meeting is ever going to be held again. But, in general, minutes should be limited to statements of decisions that were made, problems that are still open and actions that need to be taken before the next meeting. One excellent technique is to assign each action item a number and attach an action item list to the minutes. This action item list can be used as the basis of the next meeting and for reports on what has happened. As each item is taken care of, or each problem is solved, it is crossed off. The number is discarded (probably until you get up to 100) so the number becomes an identifier of the problem. By putting next to each item the date on which it was originally brought up, one also gets some feel for progress that is being made.

How Is Your Meeting Performance?

Look at your calendar for the last month and see how many different meetings you were in. Analyze what you believed was the purpose of the meeting in Maier and Hayes' terms. Evaluate the meeting in terms of your own feelings about its effectiveness. Could it have been shorter? Should it have been longer? Were the right people there? Did you have all the facts in hand? Was the meeting just a reshuffling of previous ideas? What could have been done to have moved it ahead? Did it meet needs in the participants that were just as important as the meeting itself? In other words, did the meeting have intrinsic value because of the interrelationships that were going on?

On the basis of this, think about your future meetings. In every Christian organization there should be a time when people at each level come together to share with one another and be informed as to what the situation is. Recent studies have shown that the number one reason for job satisfaction is a feeling of "being in" on what is going on. Analyze the need for regular meetings with your subordinates and superiors at which time they can have a portion of your time. Many times this will save you from interruptions during other times. Schedule problem-solving meetings far enough in advance so that the people can come prepared for them.

Evaluating Meetings

There are a number of ways of evaluating the effectiveness of meetings. Some groups have one person who is sometimes called a "Fair Communicator." His task is to insure that during the meeting people have an opportunity to be heard and that accurate communication is taking place. The same kind of person can be used as an evaluator of the meeting, or to lead the group through an evaluation of the meeting. By setting aside ten minutes at the end of any meeting and then asking the group to evaluate its own performance, both as to leadership and participation in the meeting, you'll be surprised at how open people may become in assessing what is going on. One really stimulating way to evaluate your performance as a leader, and others' performance as participants in a meeting, is to use the closed circuit videotape machines that are becoming more and more popular and do a video on the entire meeting. A review of the tape by the group together will reveal all kinds of things! What the world is all about is people.

What organizations are about is people coming together to perform a task outside themselves. What meetings are about is helping those people discuss together how they can more effectively accomplish their task. They are worth all the attention we can give them.

A Meeting Planner

In Figure 10 we have reproduced a "meeting planner" that you might find a useful tool for yourself or others. Notice that the planner starts at the point where every meeting should start, namely, the *purpose*. Provision is made for both the short-term and long-range purpose. Given the purpose, the next step should be the procedure that one is going to follow in carrying out the meeting. What kind of methods are going to be employed, what kind of tools will be necessary. At this point one can decide on people; who should do the presenting, who should be participants.

With this data in hand it is now time to plan the schedule and the facility.

And don't forget evaluation. After you've used this form to lay out the meeting that you are going to have, go back later and evaluate, then decide what you're going to do "next time."

Date _____

PURPOSE

Short Term

Long Range

PROCEDURE

Methods

Tools

PEOPLE

Presenting

Participating

PROGRAM

Schedule

Facility

PROGRESS

Evaluation

Next Time . . .

Figure 10

29.

May I Interrupt a Moment?

How many times have you heard that phrase in the past few days? Interruptions come in all shapes and sizes, but most of them are generated by people. There is the out of town visitor who "just stopped by to say hello" and is really planning to spend the afternoon with you. There are those phone calls (especially the long distance ones) which seem so demanding. More often than not it's one of your peers or subordinates who needs just "a quick piece of information," or who has stopped by to check up on the latest office rumor. Or perhaps for you it is your secretary who passes along that long line of interruptions, all waiting to be the next up.

But interruptions are not just limited to the office, are they? Just about the time that you are ready to sit down to a leisurely dinner, the telephone starts to ring, and what was supposed to be a delightful time of family interaction turns out to be a relay race between the telephone and the dinner table.

Of course some people are in the business of being interrupted. The simplest example would be the person who mans the information desk in any organization, public or private. The typical work lead-man, or the lower level supervisor, is also bound to be interrupted. The people he is working with expect him to be a source of information on what to do next.

But what about the Christian executive or pastor (who probably needs greater executive skills than any other person)? How is he to avoid the harassment of continual interruptions so that he can get on with the task to which he believes he has been called?

Why Do Interruptions Happen?

Let us begin by taking a look at why interruptions occur. Probably number one on our list would be the simple fact that other people need information. They have a real need to have more data so that they can get on with their job, or they are faced with an unexpected problem which has stumped them and which prohibits them from moving further until they have found an answer. If you are the one who has the answer, you are the one to interrupt.

Included in this list of interrupters are not only your subordinates and your peers, but also your superiors. The oil of all organizational machinery is information. If it is not applied at the right time in the right place, wheels will begin to squeak, and gears will begin to grind.

One of the main interrupters for many executives is his own secretary. If she is not guilty of trying to get information for herself, many times she has not learned how to protect her boss from the wrong kind of interruptions.

Another reason that people interrupt is that they just want fellowship, or information which will ease the tension of some problem that is filling their life. Most of us are well aware of the fact that when unexpected visitors drop by, they seldom get around to the real reason for their calling until about two minutes before they're ready to leave!

One source of interruptions that many of us seldom

identify is the fact that we interrupt ourselves! We start doing a task, when suddenly a new thought pops into our mind, or a question arises which needs answering. Before we think, we reach for the telephone, seek out our answer, and then, as we attempt to return to our work, find that we have completely lost our train of thought.

Another reason that people interrupt is that they have nothing else to do. Whether they are passing through town, or just passing down the hall, your open door is a welcome invitation to come in and pass the time of day.

Where to Begin

So much for the why of interruptions. What can be done to get them under control? As we have stated so often, the place to begin is with your *goals* and *priorities*. What comes first in your life? What is it that you want to accomplish, not only tomorrow, but today? If we have not decided why we are doing what we are doing and where it fits on our list of priorities, there is no way of judging whether what we are doing at the moment is more important than the unexpected interruption. So start with your goals. Start each day with a list of things that you want to accomplish that day. Compare these against the time needed for the other events on your calendar, and find out how much time you are going to have for interruptions if they do come. And then start applying some of the suggestions that we have listed below.

How to Control Interruptions

Interruptions from subordinates are the easiest to handle. (After all, you are supposed to be the one in charge!) The way to keep your subordinates from interrupting you is to set standard checkpoints for each task in which they are involved—times when they are going to report progress to you and discuss obstacles to overcome. Innumerable interruptions from your subordinates are an indication that they don't know what to do, and that therefore not enough time has been spent together in planning. Make sure that each of your subordinates gives you a written description of the task that he is supposed to accomplish and checkpoints that he is going to use along the way. Then set up regular meetings with those who need them. If you continue to be interrupted, ask your subordinate why the particular problem cannot wait until your next regular meeting. If it can't, then schedule more checkpoint times.

What about a Standard Day?

This logically leads to the idea of a "standard day" or a "standard week." Set down specific times each day when you are not going to receive any calls, for instance, when you are going to be working on the mail. Also schedule times when you will return calls, and maintain faith with your callers by doing so promptly. Put in your standard day or week meetings with your subordinates, peers, and superiors, and then leave in times when you are going to be *available for interruptions*. As you let others know about your standard day or standard week, they will soon learn when they can get to you directly and when you are ready to receive their questions or problems.

Open Door?

This leads directly to the question of whether you should have an "open door policy." In our own experience we have found that the open or closed door is an excellent communication device. When you sincerely are trying to avoid interruptions, close the door. When you are ready to receive interruptions, have the door open as a sign that they are welcome. Just make sure that there are times when your door *is* open. J. B. Phillips' translation of James 1:2 might be appropriate here: "When all kinds of trials and temptations crowd into your lives, my brothers, don't resent them as intruders, but welcome them as friends!"

Visitors

Suppose that an unexpected visitor does arrive unannounced, either from across the country or from across the hall. What can you do to reduce the impact of such interruptions? The first thing to do, as quickly as possible, is to establish whether the person has a real, immediate need. There is a tension in every Christian organization between getting the work done and caring for people. If your visitor is having a spiritual or emotional crisis, and you're the one who can help, perhaps this is the time to put people before the task.

Welcome people with a *positive* indication of how much time you have: "Bill, it's so good to see you! I have thirty minutes before my next commitment. What's happening with you . . ." Don't get trapped into lengthening the interruption by delving in your own set of pet stories. Look for the need in your visitor, and attempt to take care of that. Near the end of the stated time, indicate that your allotted time is ending, and ask if there are some other things that need to be discussed before you have to draw the meeting to a close. Stand up as you do this, and remain standing until the final greeting. If it is someone that you haven't seen in some time, this would be an appropriate time to pray for each other before he goes.

Group Similar Kinds of Work

Another key to help avoiding interruptions (yours and

others' is to group similar types of work. Group your outgoing phone calls at certain times during the day so that you don't interrupt yourself. Group times when you will receive incoming calls, or when you will be sure to return them. Don't be tyrannized by long-distance calls. Treat them as you would local calls.

Group other things too, such as letter writing and meetings so that you don't interrupt yourself.

Training Others

Training your secretary and your subordinates, and encouraging the training of your peers and superiors in the art of avoiding interruptions, is a good investment. Discuss with your secretary what words she can use to politely find out how critical is that incoming phone call, and how she can solicit information from the caller that will help her assess whether she should interrupt you. (For ourselves, we feel that there are two kinds of people who should always be put directly through: our superiors and members of our family, but make certain your family members don't make this a habit!) This means that your secretary, as well as your subordinates, need to have a good picture of your schedule. Many executives give their staff a copy of their weekly or monthly schedule and encourage members of their staff to exchange schedules themselves.

Enlist Volunteers

If you are in a volunteer organization, many times you can train part-timers to handle interruptions. Setting up an information center, either a telephone extension or a separate line, which is manned by volunteers, can go a long way to handling many routine questions that may come into the executive's office because people don't know where else to go.

Interruptions at Home

Many Christian executives, especially pastors, find that they have as many interruptions at home as they do in the office. If you don't want to take calls during mealtime or other family times, buy a mechanical telephone answering device (approximately $130) which will permit you to tell people when you will call back and at the same time can receive recorded messages. Some pastors leave the speaker portion of such devices on so they can hear who is calling and get back to them immediately if they need to.

Environment

Examine the environment in which you are working. Is it conducive to interruptions? Is your desk or office right near some mainstream of office traffic flow? What about the way your desk is set up within your office? Is it easy for a person to distract you from what you are doing just by standing in the doorway? Rearrange your office situation to cut down on the chance of interruptions, and at the same time to permit people to know when you are available (such as leaving your door open).

But if changing the office layout won't do it, if the number of telephone and personal interruptions remains high, then maybe the best solution is to put yourself in a *different* environment. Many executives have discovered that working at home or away from the office one day a week is a very effective way of getting large amounts of creative work done. You don't always have to go home. Perhaps there's another room or office that you can hide in while telling your secretary to let people know that, "He is out of the office right now, but I expect him back at such-and-such a time." (Never put your secretary in a position of not knowing where you are. Someone should also always know where you are located, even if you can't be reached.)

Life-style

Perhaps the greatest tool that you can use is your own life-style. As you organize your subordinates, having standard days, leaving time for others' problems, and prayerfully trying to regularly reassess your goals, you will communicate to others the kind of a person you are and help them relate to you.

30.

What to Do with the Mail?

This is a problem that probably annoys the mission or denominational executive more than the average pastor. In spite of increased postal rates it doesn't appear that there is going to be any slackening of the flood of envelopes that seems to pour forth from some huge uncheckable letter-writing machine. In the Western world the written word has tremendous power. It is concrete, repeatable, and retrievable. And though there is no guarantee that it is either accurate or truthful, it remains one of the most effective tools of communication. The problem is one of information overload. We know we need some of it. But which "some"? And how do we ever find time for what we *need* to read?

Martin Mailshuffler

It is Monday afternoon. The time is 1:30 P.M. Martin has been sitting at his desk for about twenty minutes taking care of some "emergencies" that were left over from the morning. His secretary walks in and deposits today's offering from the postal service in the in-basket. Martin is immediately interested. There is a certain excitement in receiving mail, particularly from some new source. But to find these gems he must first sort out the chaff. Martin already has a number of piles of papers from last week's arrivals stacked in five more or less neat piles on his desk. Now he goes through the mail, reading the letters and memos and putting them in the "to-be-answered" pile or the "I-will-have-to-discuss-with" pile. Most of the second, third, or fourth class letters go in the "later" pile, while the magazines and other periodicals join one of the two mounting stacks he has mentally labeled "read sometime" and "save." The entire process takes about a half hour. At the end of the time no real work has been done.

Martin now calls in his secretary, Miss Harried, and, picking up the "to-be-answered" pile, begins to dictate. During this time the telephone rings four times. Three of the calls Miss Harried could have handled, but because she is with Martin, he takes the calls while she sits trying to decipher her shorthand. One hour later she leaves Martin's office with replies to eight letters and a big question mark as to how she is going to get the rest of the day's work done.

That night Martin stuffs all the piles into a bulging briefcase. Some he will read tonight after the kids have gone to bed. Most he will lug back to the office the next morning and place back on the top of the desk.

How Do You Do It?

If this illustration seems a bit overdrawn, it is intentionally so. If it doesn't, you're in trouble.

The problem of mail overload can be helped by some basic techniques, but many times it is a symptom of a much more serious problem—ill-defined goals or wrong practices.

We'll start by describing one ideal system (there are

probably many others) and then try to point out some of the things that might stand in the way of realizing the ideal.

Start with the Secretary

Let her make the first screening. There is some mail *you* should see. There is some mail someone else should see (even, perhaps, though it is addressed to you), and there is some mail no one in the organization should see. (It goes immediately to the circular file.)

Next, let your secretary decide as to how soon you should see what. Some memos, telephone messages or letters demand immediate action on your part. Others need only be handled before the end of the day. A larger number should be handled this week. The rest may be saved for reading or review times.

Mark Action Items

The secretary should mark or underline appropriate paragraphs and items which require your action. If there are some things in the letter that she has already handled (requests for literature, information, copies to someone else), she should note these in the margin. In some cases she can even type a reply and attach it to the letter for your signature.

Items that need immediate action can be placed in a "look at now" folder and be placed near the center of your desk, while the next can go in the in-basket. This assures her that you will be aware of important items, but reduces the number of interruptions.

Use a Dictating Machine

It is nice to have a secretary who can take shorthand at 120 words a minute. But save that for when you need it.

Your task at this point is to keep the information system moving. Having another person present while you're doing it is just not the way. So use a dictating machine.

Look at the many excellent cassette dictating machines that are coming on the market. They have good fidelity and are reasonably priced. But make certain the *transcriber* your secretary uses has (1) a way for you to indicate corrections or additions, (2) speed control, (3) automatic backup and forward foot control, and (4) good clarity. For you, the small cassette recorders are great for trips, but have a more versatile machine in the office.

Read It Once and Act

This is the key to effective handling of mail. What are your options?

- Scrawl an answer on the body of the letter or memo and send it on its way back to the sender. (You can always make a copy for file.)
- Attach a handwritten note, giving someone else instructions on how to handle. (There are standard forms you can buy for this.)
- Dictate an answer. Make certain you put the original letter in a dictation folder so the secretary can get the address accurately.
- Ask for previous correspondence so you can get a complete picture.
- Send it to a pending file with a date when you need to see it again. This is particularly useful if you need more information before you can respond or you just need to be reminded. Read it and note where to file it or who else should see it.

But the key is to read it only once and take action. Don't shuffle paper.

Back to the Secretary

Have some agreed-to time limit on how long you will allow dictation to pile up. This will help you make the decision on whether to dictate a memo or write one by hand. Work this out with your secretary. (See chapter 23.) Avoid rough drafts. Encourage your secretary to keep trying to go direct to final copy. It's a hard learning process, but worth a lot of time once it is learned. Ask her where she's having trouble understanding you. If you are forgetting to spell proper names or put in punctuation, get one of the manuals many dictating machine companies provide.

Back to You

Should you read the letters you sign? If you have a good secretary, the answer is "seldom." If you know what you want to say, and she understands what you said, why read it again? Of course, there are times when you want to be extremely careful or precise and seeing it in final form is a must.

If you're not sure what to say, it's a good idea to dictate a very rough copy or just a series of ideas from which you can later dictate a final draft.

Will It Work?

Not if you don't have your goals and priorities straight, and not if you are unable to communicate them to your secretary (and the rest of your staff). You can't do everything everyone wants you to do. For certain you can't read everything the world would like you to read. You can't even read all the things you'd *like* to read (let alone do all the things you'd like to do). What is it going to be? What are you going to delegate? How are you going to train others so you are able to delegate?

The very exercise of deciding what you are going to

read and what you are not will help you to clarify your goals.

Many Christian executives and pastors start out as a one-man office. As the work expands, they forget that they can only grow as they give pieces of the task to others. If you still have a compulsion to know what's happening, set up a "read file" with copies of everything others in your office write, either for you or for themselves. Each week have your secretary give you a folder of last week's outgoing mail. In this way you can monitor what is happening, take corrective action where needed and hopefully disengage yourself from what you have delegated to others.

What If You Don't Have a Secretary?

We have suggested that the secretary do what Martin Mailshuffler was doing with two additions—diverting some mail to others and throwing some away. But what if you have no secretary?

Find someone, even a volunteer, to do the initial screening process. Here we are addressing Christian *leaders.* You can't be a leader if you haven't got time to lead. When we spent four weeks in management seminars in South Africa, we found that more pastors there had an assistant pastor than had a secretary. We'd vote for the secretary. Does that make you more important? Not in God's eyes. Rather it should reflect the kind of support you need for your role.

Some Other Tips

- Take a speed reading course and learn how to pace yourself for different kinds of reading.

- Keep letters as short as possible. They're expensive.

- Develop standard replies for repetitive kinds of problems and let your secretary compose for you.

- Block out times to handle the mail and protect them. Don't mix phone calls with letter writing. It distracts your train of thought.

- Use the telephone. Compared to the cost of letters, it grows cheaper every year.

- Plan ahead blocks of reading time (trips, carpools, etc.) when you can get at the necessary things you need to absorb.

31.

Would You Like

to Serve on a Committee?

Dr. Robert Munger, Professor of Evangelism at Fuller Theological Seminary in Pasadena, California, has devoted weekends during the school year to leading "renewal teams" at different churches in the area. One of the questions that is usually asked during a debriefing time with the offical church board is something like this: "Since serving on a church board do you feel that your spiritual life has improved or declined?" Dr. Munger reports that usually over 80 percent of the people respond that their spiritual vitality has been going downhill ever since they have been serving on a board or a committee. What's the problem? Why is it that committees have such a poor reputation? Can we do away with them?

Why Have a Committee?

There are really some very good reasons for having a committee. We may need a committee when:

- There is more work to do than one person can accomplish.

- We need special expertise or experience to bring to bear on a problem.

- Representation of a variety of opinions is needed in order to arrive at a representative decision.

Committees are formed to:
- Give policy oversight to part of the organization such as board of Christian education, salary committee, worship committee.

- To accomplish a task, like a banquet committee, a building committee.

- To solve a problem, such as parking congestion or cost control. (And, of course, sometimes the "problem" is that no individual wants to handle the hot potato by himself.)

- To air different viewpoints and make recommendations, like a constitutional committee.

What Kind of a Committee Should You Have?

The word "committee" is used rather loosely, and perhaps this is why it seems to mean so many different things to so many different people. Committees break down into basically two kinds, standing committees and committees that are designed to dissolve at a certain date. The latter are sometimes called task forces or commissions. (Probably the trouble with a lot of committees is that they are still standing when they should have had a victory celebration and a termination ceremony!)

Committees Can Be Dangerous

Many Christian organizations are organized around a committee structure. Very often a local church will have a worship committee, a board of Christian education, a missionary committee, a finance committee, etc. As we pointed out in chapter 11 on Self-Renewal, all too often

the *structure* becomes the governing element of the organization and prohibits the organization from reshaping
itself towards new and changing goals. One church we
know of has attempted to overcome this by having only
one committee (a board of elders) and then doing everything else (including the Sunday school) through a series of
task forces, each of which has a termination date.

Another danger of standing committees is that they
have a tendency to become isolated from the mainstream
of the thought of the rest of the organization.

Committees Have Great Value

But, before we start trying to do away with all committees, we should recognize that the committee is a special
grouping which has great power for good. If they are properly organized and led, they can permit a degree of involvement by members of the organization that is not
possible in any other way. They can promote a sense of
oneness and inclusiveness within a group that is extremely
helpful for morale. Furthermore, for many types of volunteer organizations they are needed to lend authority to
the direction of the entire organization.

How to Start a Committee

Almost always a committee is formed on the basis of
perceived need of some individual or group. Sometimes
the "need" is for someone to get off the hook, "Let's send
that to committee . . ." But the effectiveness of a committee can sometimes stand or fall on how clear a job description and mandate the committee is given at the
beginning. Whoever is establishing the committee should
give a clear statement of (1) its purpose, (2) any specific
goals that it should have, (3) to whom and how often it is
to report and the form that the report is to take, (4) the

limits of its authority, proposals to take action, spend money or expand its membership, (5) the date, if any, by which it is to include its actions and/or be dissolved.

Most committees must proceed through the standard divisions of management: staffing, organizing, training, work division, work assignment, conferring, consensus, reporting and/or acting and reporting.

If the appointing individual or group will recognize this, then he can set up checkpoints along the way at which he can ask for reports back from the committee as to how far they have proceeded in their assignment.

Who Should Serve on the Committee?

This is the key question. Many committees have formed which never seem to get off the ground. People continually ask us, "How do you motivate people to do what they're supposed to do?" The answer, of course, lies in finding someone who is already motivated. *Everyone is motivated toward something.* Our task in life is to match up people's motivation with tasks. This is where the concept of goal ownership is very important. Many times there will exist within the organization those who have a special burden for the task or problem that the committee is charged with, and these are the obvious people with whom to begin.

How Many People Should Be on the Committee?

This will have a great deal to do with how much work the committee has to do and how broad a spectrum of opinion is required. In volunteer organizations, such as local churches, representation is extremely important. A committee which does not find a broad representation between "old" and newer members, pragmatists and reflectors, and is not sensitive to the informal information system and power structure within the organization, will always have difficulty. Many times a committee is formed much too hastily. It would have been far better to have spelled out the parameters of representation and then asked someone who was motivated toward serving on it to make recommendations that fit these parameters.

Of course, if the committee has been formed to accomplish a specific task, such as work with an architect on designing a new building, then special expertise is going to be needed. But, again, make sure that representation is not overlooked.

It is very helpful if the appointing individual or group will try to think through the type of problems that the committee will face in the course of its life and *then* consider the different types of individuals who will be needed at subsequent phases in the life of the committee. Recognize, too, that the committee may require different types of people at different times, and where appropriate ask people to serve on it in special capacities for a short period of time.

How to Make a Committee Effective

Too often a committee is appointed for a particular purpose, but as the weeks and months go by, it becomes obvious that the committee is not going to act. The problem probably emanated because of oversight in giving the committee a proper charge. However, it could also be that no follow-up system was instituted. Follow-up is important, both for those for whom the committee is working and for the committee itself. Such an interchange with the leadership of the organization, either through personal contact or through correspondence, gives both sides a sense of direction.

A very good way to get a committee moving is to instruct it to spend its first meeting spelling out the dimensions of the problem it is to solve and to then outline a rough plan for accomplishing its task. Many times this will have to be a plan for planning. In other words, the committee will not know the details of what it's going to do, but should be able to <u>set down some guidelines,</u> by which time it will have completed a plan. It is important here to make sure the committee understands what kind of feedback the governing body wants to know is what has happened! The first thing that any governing body or leader wants to know is *what decisions* do you want it (him) to make. The second thing they want to know is *what problems* the committee faces; the third thing they want to know is what the committee *plans to do* in the days that lie ahead.

A fast response to any verbal or written report from the committee, indicating appreciation and assistance, will do a great deal to encourage the committee towards its task.

Meetings

It is important to remember that the purpose of a committee is not to "meet." Too often committee work is thought of only in terms of meetings. In chapter 28, we discussed the entire area of effective meetings, so we won't repeat that here, except to say that every effort should be made on the part of the committee's leadership to show progress and to move the group toward specific steps in the goal. The project checklist that was given in chapter 6 is very helpful in making committee assignments and showing people where they are with reference to the rest of the group.

Committee Work

The real work of most committees should be done not at the meeting, but in other places. Here it is important that people have clear assignments and they understand how these assignments relate to other people. The chairman needs to be particularly sensitive to the need to give written assignment when necessary to people within your organization, be it a local church or some other structure, know that you will consistently return their calls or that you are usually available at a certain time to receive calls, they will get in the habit of calling at that time.

Use the telephone at certain times instead of a letter. The cost of producing a typewritten letter will usually far exceed the cost of a long distance telephone call, particularly if you have organized your thoughts ahead of time. (On the other hand, when you have to notify a large number of people about a routine situation, such as a forthcoming meeting, it is probably much less time-consuming to mail out a written notification well in advance. This also makes it easy for the people receiving the information to keep it as a reminder.)

Use the telephone in emergencies and when you need information right away. For example, if the need for one piece of information is blocking further communication with a group of people, the telephone call is an effective way to get things moving again.

How to Use the Telephone

Organize your thoughts ahead of time. Jot down points you want to cover on a 3-by-5-inch card or a slip of paper. If you're going to need information during the course of the phone call, make sure that paper is available.

Always introduce yourself unless there is absolutely no doubt that the person answering the phone will know immediately who you are. If appropriate, state the reason you are calling. Many times by just leaving your request for information you can find out what you want to know without getting to the person you were originally trying to reach.

Training

Don't overlook the fact that very many people just don't know how to work on a committee. There should be times of reflection when the committee itself evaluates its progress.

And don't overlook the fact that for a standing committee, such as a board of Christian education, training new members should become a key part of the task of the committee. As they are rotated onto the committee, they should be carefully briefed as to what has happened in the past, what are the committee's goals and the details of their particular assignment.

Finally, don't overlook the need for personal rewards on the part of those who serve on committees. Give recognition wherever possible. Think of ways such as letters of appreciation, mention in the organization news bulletin, special supper or dinner, or even some small gift that indicates the organization appreciates the tremendous amount of work that has gone into the committee.

32.

Telephone—Friend or Foe?

What's Happening?

You hear it everywhere. "These are busy days." "So much is happening at every turn." "There seems to be so little time." Why is this so? Primarily, the reason is the number of "personal intersections" is rising all the time. The number of people who can touch your life and whose life *you* can touch is increasing rapidly. This in turn is due to two things: First, there just are more people in the world. Second, Western technology makes possible through transportation and communication many more such personal intersections.

Telephone—Friend or Foe?

Certainly one of the greatest potential contributors to personal intersections is the telephone. Western society is built around its use. Local churches in modern America would have to develop an entirely new style of community life without it. Christian organizations would have to restructure themselves dramatically. For the telephone is at the heart of the *informal* communication system. And it is the informal communication system that is really the lifeblood of a society. "What time is the church meeting

Tuesday night?" "When can we get together for lunch to talk about Joe's proposal?" "How can we get in touch with Mary's mother to tell her that she has had an accident?" "I wonder how Mom and Dad are getting along?" These are all questions that can be easily answered by the telephone. And they are all questions which most of us ask at one time or another.

On the other hand, the telephone may be the vehicle through which we receive many *unwelcome* questions. "Bill, can you come down to my office for a few minutes?" "Mary, we're having a meeting of the women's society tomorrow night, and we need you there." "Could you speak to our Clipper Club meeting a week from Thursday night?" "We are making a survey of people whose homes are not now heated by natural gas: can I take a few minutes of your time?"

It's Just a Tool

And like all tools it can be misused. (There are no sinful things, only sinful people!) How do we make it our *servant* and not our enemy? How do we keep from misusing it in a way that will be detrimental to other people?

One of the greatest advantages of the telephone is, of course, its ease of use. If you can talk and can master the instructions for dialing (or punching) theoretically that's all the training you need. Herein lies the greatest problem. Using the telephone takes a great deal more skill than most of us believe. What skills do you and the people in your organization need in order to make the telephone a tool for the furtherance of the Kingdom rather than a time-wasting tyrant?

Teach People When to Use It

Use it during specified times during the day by group-

268

ing outgoing and incoming telephone calls together. This will not only make it more convenient for you (you can look forward to a time when you're going to originate and receive calls), but it will also make it more convenient for those who work for you (particularly a secretary) and those who are trying to get in touch with you.

Have a time in mind when the person can call you back if they are not available at that particular moment. This will save them (and you) a lot of frustration.

If you are frustrated by your inability to get past someone's officious-sounding secretary and it really is a matter of urgency, try the phrase "Would you please interrupt him and tell him Mr. So-and-so has an urgent problem?" This puts the responsibility back on your own shoulders and helps the secretary who may be caught in the dilemma of not knowing what to do.

How to Answer the Telephone

In almost any organizational setting you should always immediately identify yourself. Don't just pick up the telephone and say, "Hello." Rather, try a warm, "This is Ted Engstrom." This does two things. It helps people from going into a long dialogue with the wrong person. It also intimates to the caller that he should introduce himself and saves embarrassment upon your part.

If someone else is answering the telephone on your behalf, make sure that they use the same form of identification. Again, don't forget that as far as the caller is concerned the way that the telephone is answered is the way *you* want it answered and is thus a reflection of you. A "Good morning, this is Ed Dayton's office" sounds somewhat nicer than "Ed Dayton's office" or a mere "Hello."

If someone is answering your telephone for you, *always*

make sure that you have a clear understanding as to whether you want to take telephone calls at this particular time. This seems to be a great problem for a lot of people who are embarrassed to have their secretaries say that they are in their office and don't want to be disturbed and yet at the same time, as a matter of Christian conscience don't want to "lie." One nice way of handling this when the caller says only "Is he there?" (note that the caller did not say who he was or why he wanted to speak), the secretary can respond "He will be available at 10 o'clock. Can I have him call you then?" This immediately places the caller in the position of having to identify himself or herself and the nature of his or her business. It also removes the difficulty that the secretary and the caller may feel if she answers the first question with "May I ask who's calling please?" For if you *are* unavailable, it may appear to the caller that you are only unavailable to *him*.

But suppose that you are ready to receive telephone calls, what should the secretary do then? If the person answering your telephone is not quite familiar with the different people who call you, he or she will need some way of helping you to ascertain whether you want to speak to this person. (For instance, your church or organization may have a policy that it never talks to salesmen over the telephone.) When in doubt, a simple, but warm, "Could I tell him (or her) the nature of your call?" will usually get further information. Train those answering the telephone to *write down the answers* to any questions they might ask. It's amazing how easy it is to forget a name. It's perfectly all right for the secretary to ask how to spell a caller's name and thus avoid further embarrassment.

Don't get trapped by the long-distance syndrome. Just because a person is calling from 2000 miles away doesn't mean that you *have* to answer. Again, take the responsibility to call back, or to tell them when they can call you back.

This is a good place to mention something that most of us have learned by now: Direct dialing is cheaper in the long run than person-to-person calls. Even though you may not get the person the first time you call, by dialing direct you can find out when they are available and make a date for the second call. You can even tell the secretary the kind of information that the person should have available when you call again.

The Telephone at Home

Perhaps you are just getting too many calls. You are finding yourself spending all of your time on the telephone. What can you do?

The first thing to do is to look at yourself. Are you the one who prolongs telephone calls? One of the helpful things that you can do here is to identify (even to people to whom you *want* to talk) what your time frame is. "Mary, I have to get back to something in five minutes, but I'm so glad you called."

If you feel that you are doing an effective job of communicating over the telephone, but you are still getting too many calls, there are a number of other things you might do. Some pastors and Christian executives find it very effective never to answer the telephone when they are home. Many times by having a list of information next to the telephone a member of the family can supply whatever information the caller wants.

Perhaps you need to coach your family when it is and when it is not acceptable for you to carry on telephone conversations. For instance, "Could he call you back? We are right in the middle of dinner" is a very appropriate response.

Don't Overlook the Answering Machine

There are now many good telephone answering devices on the market. Normally you can purchase one and have it installed for less than $150. (Check with your telephone company as to special requirements.) The answering machine has some excellent advantages: First, you don't have to answer the telephone if you are in the midst of something else. The recorded message can ask the one calling to leave their telephone number and name and any brief message which you can pick up at your convenience. Second, you can be assured that there will always be "someone" to pick up your calls even when you are away from the house or the office. Third, you will discover that most people are quite pleased to leave their message with the answering machine. At least they *know* that they have gotten in touch with you, and if you have a reputation of being a person who calls back this will usually satisfy their need.

Other Ways

There are other more expensive ways of handling an overload of phone calls: You can arrange for the telephone company to have them automatically switched to another number where you can have a volunteer or someone else answer. Or you can use a telephone answering service. One thing that you can do (which the phone company won't like) is just leave the telephone off the hook.

And last, think about just letting it ring. It's great discipline.

Where to Go for More Help

Make sure that you call your telephone company and ask them what kind of training they have available for your staff. It is usually free of charge. They will also have booklets.

PART FIVE

Christian Excellence

33.

Christian Excellence

In 1961 John Gardner, who was then head of the Carnegie Corporation, and was subsequently to move on to prominent roles of leadership in HEW and Common Cause, wrote a book with the simple title, *Excellence* (Harper and Row).

The book was subtitled, "Can We Be Equal and Excellent Too?" In this book, Gardner was attacking the idea that it is almost undemocratic to excel at something over your fellow man.

Gardner was on the right track. We need to excel. And yet, Christians also fall into this same trap of believing that no one should be better than someone else. We become uneasy with the idea of having the best, being the best, or doing that which is outstanding. In our thinking too often we don't mind "excellence" if we can shift responsibility for it onto the Lord. "The Lord has really blessed his ministry," or "The Lord really gave him great gifts." But we may become suspicious if someone is praised directly for doing an excellent job.

There are some real tensions here, and they work themselves out in strange ways:

- We once visited a beautiful chapel on a new church

campus. In contrast to three obviously expensive chandeliers was a hand-drawn Sunday school attendance chart taped on the foyer wall. $1500 for chandeliers, but the best they could do to communicate what was happening to *people* was a crude graph.

- Another time, World Vision was criticized for purchasing first quality plumbing for a new building, a long-term investment that has paid good dividends, but at the time seemed "too good" to some.

- In contrast is the pride we exhibit when a *Christian* makes the "big time" in athletics or politics. For some reason it's all right to praise a man for other *non-Christian* things!

A Problem of Theology

Part of our problem is just defective theology. Most of us cannot live with the biblical (paradoxical) truth that God is doing it all—he is in all and through all, and the parallel, and just as completely incomprehensible, truth—man is the one who has not only been given complete responsibility for his actions, but is *commanded* to act. All of this is part of our tension in theology and life. We constantly struggle with the concept of operating a business and a ministry. They do not conflict; both are vital.

But we are called to excellence. And we are called to set standards of excellence for ourselves and all men. In Philippians 1:10 Paul prays that we may have the ability to approve those things that are excellent.

"Be ye perfect as I am perfect" is the standard. But where to begin? Does a call to excellence mean a call to excellence in *everything*?

Colossians 3:17 admonishes us "and whatever you do, in word or deed, do everything in the name of the Lord

Jesus, giving thanks to God the Father through him." No higher standard could be found.

And yet most of us must admit that there are large segments of our life where this is not our experience. What's the answer? How do we as Christian leaders apply these criteria?

Let's start with some definitions.

Excellence Is a Measure

First: Excellence is a measure. It demands definition. One of the trite replies of our day when asked how we like something or how well something is going, is "Compared to what?"

But excellence is like that. It assumes a standard.

And conversely excellence assumes inferiority. It assumes there's a way of doing or being something that is

• less than the best.

• less than what it could be.

• less than worthwhile.

Excellence Assumes a Goal

Second: Excellence assumes a goal, an objective. Excellence demands that we think beyond dreams, think beyond concepts; that we think into reality—in terms of what can be, what should be.

Excellence Assumes Priorities

Third: Excellence assumes priorities. It not only has to do with doing one thing well, but is concerned with a choice between goals. There are some *goals* that are less worthy, less honoring to God, goals that fall short of all that God intends us to be. It is not that there is one right way for all men, but rather that a potential for excellence in *some* area lies in all men. We are called to live a life in which we need to do many things to live our life, but within which we are called to do some things with excellence. Certainly to excel in prayer. Perhaps to excel in one book of the Bible or to exercise one gift to its fullest potential. (Some of us have great gifts, but we are too lazy to unwrap them.)

Excellence Is a Process

Fourth: Excellence is more of a process than an achievement. Similarly, life is a process; management is a process. There are times in history when we can look at an individual or event and pronounce it *excellent*, but it is continually pressing on that marks the man dedicated to excellence.

> Brethren, I do not consider that I have made it my own; but one thing I do, forgetting what lies behind and straining forward to what lies ahead, I press on toward the goal for the prize of the upward call of God in Christ Jesus. (Phil. 3:13–14).

Excellence Should Be a Style of Life

Fifth: Excellence has to do with a style of life. Know yourself. What is your style? What can it be? People are tremendously different. They have different gifts. They have different callings. There are: outgoing and introspective people, thinkers and doers, leaders and followers, logical and intuitive persons, teachers and learners.

Some people are ahead of their time, some are behind. Few are musical geniuses, most are not. Some are great preachers, some are not. Some are conceivers of grand ideas, others are people of small detail.

But for each of us, excellence demands that we be true to the best that God has placed within us. My style of life should be one of excellence. The Christian can adopt nothing less as his goal.

Excellence Has to Do with Motivation

Sixth: Excellence has to do with motivation. Excellence is not achieved easily. The first 80 percent of an excellent solution comes easy. The next 15 percent is difficult. Only the highly motivated person reaches 100 percent.

There is a joy in such achievement that is an all-too-rare experience for most of us. One of the mysteries of living is that the goal which is achieved easily brings little inner satisfaction or reward. Old victories will serve for old age, but before that I must forget what lies behind and press on to the high calling that lies ahead.

Think big! Believe a big God! Remember that "God is greater . . . !"

Excellence Assumes Accountability

Seventh: Excellence assumes accountability, either to our own inner standard or the standard of the group. Oh, how we Christians have so often missed that!

- Excellence is a measurement, and that assumes a standard of accountability. Yes or no. Make it or not.

- Excellence demands a goal, and that's sticking your neck out to others.

- Excellence demands priorities, and that's telling people what comes first in your life.

- Excellence is a process, and that means continually checking progress.

- Excellence has to do with style and that means deciding what gifts God has given me and how I should be responsible for those gifts.

- Excellence has to do with motivation, and that's what it's all about!

How Do We Respond to the Goal of Excellence?

1. Sort out your goals. You can't do everything. You can't be everything. And that's all right.

2. Of those goals you believe you must push toward, decide which have *top* priority. Do these with excellence.

3. Decide who you are and what you are, or, paradoxically, decide how God made you and what he wants you to be. Do that with excellence. It was said of Jesus, "Behold, he does all things well." Can we do less?

4. As we seek Christian excellence, keep it in perspective. Some things are more excellent than others. Before that verse in Philippians 1:10 Paul tells us how we will be able to judge that which is excellent.

"And it is my prayer that your love may abound more and more, with knowledge and all discernment, so that you may approve what is excellent, and may be pure and blameless for the day of Christ, filled with the fruits of righteousness which come through Jesus Christ, to the glory and praise of God" (Phil. 1:9).

The *purpose* is glory and praise of God. The *goal* is excellence.

Note that the steps to the goal are knowledge and discernment thoroughly mixed together with abounding love.

The *measurement* is the fruits of righteousness.

The *power* comes through Jesus Christ.

All glory to Him!

Life is a leaf of paper white
Whereon each one of us may write
His word or two, and then comes night.

Greatly begin! though thou hast time
But for a line, be that sublime . . .
Not failure, but low aim, is crime.
                    James Russell Lowell

Bibliography

Basset, Glen A. *Management Styles in Transition*. American Management Association, 1966.

Becker, Esther, and Anders, Evelyn. *The Successful Secretary's Handbook*. Harper & Row, 1971.

Bennis, Warren. *Organization Development, Its Nature, Origin, and Prospects*. Addison Wesley, 1969.

Cook, Fred S., and Forti, Lenore S. *Professional Secretary's Handbook*. Dartnell, 1971.

Dayton, Edward R. *God's Purpose/Man's Plans*. World Vision's Missions Advanced Research and Communication Center (MARC), 1974.

_____ *Tools for Time Management*. Zondervan, 1974.

Dooher, Joseph, ed. *Effective Communication on the Job*. American Management Association, 1956.

Drucker, Peter. *The Practice of Management*. Harper & Row, 1954.

_____ *The Effective Executive*. Harper & Row, 1966.

_____ *Management: Tasks, Responsibilties, Practices*. Harper & Row, 1974.

Engel, James, and Norton, H. Wilbert. *What's Gone Wrong with the Harvest?* Eerdmans, 1975.

Engstrom, Ted W., *The Making of a Christian Leader*. Zondervan, 1976.

Engstrom, Ted, and Mackenzie, Alec. *Managing Your Time*. Zondervan, 1967.

Ewing, David. *The Human Side of Planning*. Macmillan, 1969.

Gardner, John. *Self Renewal*, Harper & Row, 1964.

_____ *Excellence.* Harper & Row, 1961.

Harris, Thomas A. *I'm OK—You're OK.* Harper & Row, 1967.

Hughes, Charles. *Goal Setting.* American Management Association, 1965.

Herzberg, F. *Work and the Nature of Man.* Cleveland World Publishers, 1966.

Kelley, Dean. *Why Conservative Churches Are Growing.* Harper & Row, 1972.

Kepner, Charles H., and Tregoe, B. B. *The Rational Manager,* McGraw-Hill, 1965.

Likert, Rensis. *The Human Organization.* McGraw-Hill, 1967.

Mackenzie, Alec. *The Time Trap.* Amacom, 1972.

Mager, Robert. *Goal Analysis.* Fearon Press, 1972.

Maier, Norman, and Hayes, John. *Creative Management.* John Wiley & Sons, 1962.

McCay, James T. *The Management of Time.* Prentice-Hall, 1959.

McLaughlin, Ray W. *Communication for the Church.* Zondervan, 1968.

Odiorne, George. *Management by Objectives.* Pitman Publishing Corporation, 1965.

Reddin, W. J. *Effective Management By Objectives: The 3D Method of MBO.* McGraw-Hill, 1971.

Schaller, Lyle. *The Change Agent.* Abingdon, 1972.

_____ *Parish Planning.* Abingdon, 1971.

_____ *The Decision-Makers*. Abingdon, 1974.

Wolff, Richard. *Man At the Top*. Tyndale, 1969.

Yaker, Henri; Osmond, Humphrey; and Cheek, Frances. *The Future of Time*. Anchor, 1972.

Index